JAPANESE CULT CINEMA

FILMS FROM THE SECOND GOLDEN AGE
SELECTED ESSAYS & REVIEWS

J M UPTON

For all cinephiles.

Copyright © 2023 by J.M. Upton

All rights reserved.

Text © 2023 by J.M. Upton

Cover & images © J.M. Upton 2023

No part of this book may be reproduced in any form or by any electronic or mechanical means, including information storage and retrieval systems, without written permission from the author, except for the use of brief quotations in a book review.

ISBN: 978-1-3999-5227-9 (pbk.)

ISBN: 978-1-3999-5228-6 (e-book)

Noctua Press®

London, UK

www.noctuapress.com

Written & Edited by J.M. Upton

Cover Design: J.M. Upton & Charles A. Cornell

INTRODUCTION

"Are you okay?" I put my hand on Ms. Terasawa's shoulder. She raised her head slowly, a look of embarrassed horror on her face. "Yes…but I can't watch this part." It was the first time I had seen a university professor of film studies react so viscerally to a movie. Up until now, we'd watched older films from the '50s and '60s. Great films with plenty of sex and violence. But this film elicited a reaction like none I'd seen from a scholar. Takashi Miike's notorious *Audition* was a cult film. Miike was part of an altogether new generation of filmmakers who set about to build upon the heritage of their golden age predecessors while remaining stylistically unique.

For the uninitiated, the first golden age of Japanese cinema began in the 1950s and lasted for almost two decades. The postwar era was also a transnational one, spawning such internationally renowned directors as Akira Kurosawa, Ishiro Honda, Yasujiro Ozu, and Seijun Suzuki. Some of the greatest and most iconic films ever made come from this period and developed a cult following internationally, including *Gojira* (1954), *Kwaidan* (1964), and *Branded to Kill* (1965.)

On the 2022 list of the top 100 movies ever, compiled by critics at *Sight & Sound*, Ozu's *Tokyo Story* (1953) came in at number four.

A BBC survey conducted in 2018 ranked Kurosawa's *Seven Samurai* (1954) as the best foreign film of all time.

Many films from this period were remade with great success. *Seven Samurai* became *The Magnificent Seven* (1960) and *Yojimbo* (1961) became *A Fistful of Dollars* (1964.) The 1970s ushered in a period of contraction. The oil crisis and the Nixon controversy in America both had a negative impact on the Japanese economy. Industrial production increased as energy usage decreased.

While the period from 1970 to the early 1990s produced many great works, including the early films of Hayao Miyazaki and new wave/underground titles like *Tetsuo* (1989) and *Violent Cop* (1989), it wasn't until the 1990s that Japan enjoyed its second boom.

This boom precisely coincides with the creation of DVD distribution labels such as Tartan's Asia Extreme (1992-2003) and The Criterion Collection (who entered the DVD market in the late 1990s) began releasing titles from Japan and marketing them as culturally important and/or cult films.When the Internet became available, film fans outside the big cities once reliant on bootleg VHS copies of the works of cult directors like Takeshi Kitano and Takashi Miike, purchased at trade shows and film conventions could now order their most significant works with the click of a button.

Simultaneously, popular Hollywood filmmakers like Quentin Tarantino openly praised then-newly released films such as *Battle Royale* (2000.) Global successes like the Academy Award-winning *Princess Mononoke* (1997) and the horror hits *Ringu* (1998), *and Audition* (1999), gave Japanese cinema what many consider to be its second golden age on the global stage. Once again, many of the best films from this era were re-made in Hollywood with Gore Verbinski's *The Ring* (2002) being the best of the bunch.

My own entry into this world started precisely at the peak, in the late 1990s in Los Angeles when films like *Cure*, and *Kikujiro* enjoyed regular play on several American satellite channels as well as screenings at the New Beverly Cinema and Nuart Theatre.

INTRODUCTION

I'll never forget the first time I saw Kyoshi Kurosawa's moody potboiler police thriller *Cure*. I was mesmerized.

The movie took me down a rabbit hole that ultimately led to more than two decades of writing about Japanese cult cinema, first as a freelance film reviewer, then as a graduate student in London, where I moved to study the medium in a more formal setting. Japanese cinema brought me to a greater understanding of Japan in general, including the nation's attitudes about sex, its indigenous religion Shintoism and how Japanese filmmakers often use symbolism which can be analyzed using western methodologies.

This collection, while in no way comprehensive of the period, includes both academic essays and selected reviews of some of my favorite titles covering the period spanning the early 1990s to the mid 2000s. Being a genre film fan, the J-horror section of this book is the longest, filled with movies featuring monsters, ghosts, zombies, murderers and mysteries.

Many of the most transnationally successful cult films from this era were created by auteurs, such as the aforementioned Kitano, Takashi Miike, and the lesser-acknowledged Shusuke Kaneko even when they were working within the confines of a previously successful film franchise or a book adaptation. For this reason, I have chosen them for inclusion.

I have deliberately left out any of the films of Hayao Miyazaki because I have nothing to add that hasn't already been written. They're great. See them. This book is meant for students and casual fans of Japanese cult films alike. It is my hope to lead you down your own cinematic rabbit hole in a considered and fun way. Similar to Sadako in the *Ringu* series of books and films whose survival depended on the copying and distribution of a video, my purpose is to propagate my love for Japanese cinema.

Tanoshi! 楽しむ

J.M. Upton

PART ONE
TAKESHI KITANO

"I do all these various activities like painting and writing, comedy and films probably because…I'm not good at any of them."

"BEAT" TAKESHI KITANO

STONE FACE, SOFT HEART

In the 1990s one name was synonymous the world over with modern Japanese cinema.

Western critics wrote of him with nearly the same reverence reserved for Akira Kurosawa and Yasjujiro Ozu and western filmmakers like Wes Anderson stole his best bits. That name is Takeshi Kitano.

Kitano Takeshi is a man of many identities including comedian, dancer, actor, writer, director, and painter. He was born in 1947, the youngest of four children. He grew up under harsh conditions in Adachi, Tokyo. His father Kikujiro was a war veteran who returned home to a life of scraping away as a painter, spending most of his meager wages on alcohol to numb his battle-born pain.

His mother Saki, an educator and factory worker, pushed her son academically. Although a bit younger compared to other post-war auteur directors, such as Nagisa Oshima (whom he would later act for) and Kinji Fukasaku, growing up in the "new" Japan would play and integral role in the development of Kitano's artistic sensibility (Standish 2005, 325.)

Despite his mother stressing the importance of a good education, Kitano did not take well to student life at Meiji University where student protests against the renewal of the U.S. Security Treaty were common, perhaps lending fuel to Kitano's internal rebellious fire. He eventually dropped out and landed a job as an elevator boy at the France Theatre in Asakusa, where he studied performance under the tutelage of Master Senzaburo Fukami.

In the 1970s he created the very successful Manzai comedy team *Two Beats* where Kitano played the dominant role of Beat Takeshi to his submissive partner Beat Kiyoshi played by Kiyoshi Kaneko. Following a very successful Television career both with and without Kaneko, Kitano branched out into motion picture acting and directing.

In 1988, he established Office Kitano, which helped to secure his reputation as an independent transnational avant-garde artist who makes films on his own terms, often mixing drama, comedy and action with the occasional musical number thrown in for good measure.

It took a while for Japanese audiences to accept the dark tone of his films, but with complete creative control, he was, within a few years, able to establish himself firmly within the pantheon of great Japanese directors in the tradition of Akira Kurosawa and Seijun Suzuki, making films that both critics and audiences would enjoy. I have chosen four from the second golden age for this book.

Kitano entered his peak period of success with the release of *Sonatine* in 1993, a bleak yet uplifting film about a bored Yakuza (Kitano) who brings together a bunch of other Yakuza on a beach in Okinawa. The film concludes with the titular character's suicide. A year later, Kitano would be involved in a motorcycle accident he referred to as "an unconscious suicide attempt," that left one side of his face paralyzed. During recovery, he took up painting and merged mediums by including his paintings within his films, making his work the ultimate expression of a singular, multi-talented artist.

In 1997, *Hana-bi* took home the Golden Lion at the 54th Venice International Film Festival. Kitano not only wrote, directed and starred in the film, he also served as editor. *Kikujiro* (1999), arguably his most personal film, was nominated for the Palme d'Or at Cannes. It deservedly won composer Joe Hisaishi the Award of the Japanese Academy for Best Music Score. It is my favorite Kitano film, not only for the wonderful absurdly childish humor, but for the themes and performances.

A few years later, Kitano received The Silver Lion for Best Director in 2003 for his remake of *Zatoichi*, a film notable for its unique handling of its beloved franchise source material.

Although I have not included films he did not direct, his most widely recognized acting role came in Kinji Fukasaku's *Battle Royale* (2000) as the jaded teacher Kitano who pits his teen students against each other in a game of survival 12 years before *The Hunger Games* got there.

Throughout his career spanning more than 50 years, he has remained an artist who creates on his own terms. He solidified this free-spirit reputation in 2018, when he left the production company he created at age 71 to "go independent." In 2023, Kitano denied rumors of his retirement, much to the delight of his western and Japanese fanbases. If his future work is half as interesting as his past work, I'm there.

HANA-BI (1997)
AKA FIREWORKS

In Japanese, the word "hana" means flower, and "bi" fire. Combined, they make the word fireworks, which blossom in the night sky, bursting forth into life, only to disappear in haste.

Similarly, *Hana-bi* is a bittersweet tale, told calmly, peppered with incredible short bursts of violence. The film tells the story of the downward spiral of Detective Nishi (Takeshi Kitano.) A formerly decorated officer of the law, his five-year-old daughter has recently died and his wife Miyuki (played by Kitano-regular Kayoko Kishimoto) is battling leukemia.

One day, Detective Horibe (Ren Osugi), Nishi's police colleague and friend since childhood, replaces Nishi on a stakeout shift so Nishi can visit Miyuki in the hospital. Horibe gets shot and suffers life-changing injuries. He will live out the remainder of his life in a wheelchair, paralyzed from the waist down.

Shortly after the shooting, one of his other colleagues is murdered in the ensuing struggle as Nishi and two other officers try to subdue Horibe's attacker in a shopping mall.

Had he done his shift as planned, his friend would be healthy and another officer would still be alive. Nishi feels incredible guilt. Not since Clint Eastwood has an actor been able to convey so much emotion with such an expressionless face. Especially when Horibe announces that his beloved wife and daughter have abandoned him. At the seaside, he tells Nishi he was thinking of buying a beret and becoming an artist but he can't afford the art supplies. A few days later, he attempts suicide.

Nishi has reached his breaking point. He retires from the force and borrows money from a gang of Yakuza. He uses the money to look after his wife at home, the dead officer's widow, and buy his friend everything he needs to become an artist, beret included.

When Nishi can no longer afford the loan payments, he buys a stolen taxi, paints it to look like a police car and robs a bank. It is the quietest bank robbery ever executed in a film. No one speaks and there's no music.

Nishi pays off his debts and takes Miyuki on a road trip. Their last together. The Yakuza follow him, demanding Nishi pay them "interest." Nishi kills them. When his former colleagues come to arrest him by the seaside, he asks for a last moment with Miyuki. The film concludes with Nishi shooting his wife and then himself offscreen. Roll credits.

It's quite possible that *Hana-bi* is the most narcissistic film in Kitano's body of work. He wrote, directed and edited the film and appears as the lead. His past, present and future (at the time of production) are in every frame. Is that a negative? Hell, no.

Each character is a different aspect of the real Kitano. In Horibe, we have a man who once lived to work. Now confined to his wheelchair, he turns to painting and drawing to give his life meaning. All the paintings created by Horibe in the film are Kitano's. Almost every time we see a character sitting against a wall, there's a Kitano behind them dwarfing the actor within the frame.

All these works were completed during and after Kitano's recovery period following the 1994 motorcycle accident that almost killed him. The pieces are wonderfully dense with detail, filled with child-like, upbeat colorful images. A stark contrast to the events playing out in Nishi's life.

Although not strictly autobiographical, the film's ending

makes it clear Kitano was still working through some personal issues when he made *Hana-bi*. He even gives one of the Yakuza a white eye patch just like the one he wore following his accident. An accident he later admitted was a suicide attempt.

Horibe, like Kitano, finds solace in his art while Nishi and his wife die together on the beach. It should feel depressing, but somehow, it's not.

Joe Hisaishi's score is anything but bleak. The locations and photography are stunning. Kitano is just about the best director in the world for tackling downbeat material abstractly, leaving audiences in a peaceful place as they exit the theatre.

Hana-bi was the film that brought Kitano international fame. Even Akira Kurosawa loved this movie.[1] A man who knew a little something about the high contrast nature of life and how to express it sublimely on film.

Hana-bi builds on the tonal foundation laid in Kurosawa's anthology film *Dreams* (1990) in the segment titled *Village of the Watermills*. Both are life-affirming in tackling the concept of the inevitably of death. Perhaps there is something to be said for the claim that the best artists suffer to become great.

ZATOICHI (2003)

I'll never forget the first time I read that Beat Takeshi was making a Zatoichi film. The image of a bleach-blonde Kitano intrigued me, but I wondered, "Do we really need another Zatoichi film?"

After all, it is a beloved Japanese franchise. A jidaigeki (period) film series that ran for 26 films with Shintaro Katsu playing the lead from 1965 to 1989, plus 100 episodes of a 1970s TV series.

Imagine if Sean Connery had played James Bond forever. There was no Roger Moore, Pierce Brosnan or Daniel Craig. Then someone new came along. Stepping into Shintaro Katsu's sandals to play the blind masseur/swordsman Ichi would be a tall order for any actor.

There was probably no filmmaker or actor in early 2000s Japan who could subvert our expectations the way Kitano could. And subvert them he, did.

Zatoichi is neither a typical Takeshi Kitano film nor a film typical of its series predecessors. It's a perfect blend of the two, composed of heaping portions of comedy, action, music and Japanese film history.

A blind swordsman masseur named Ichi wanders into a town besieged by several warring factions of Yakuza, each shaking down the townsfolk for "protection money" to the point of poverty. He befriends lonely Aunty Oume (Michiyo Okusu) and her nephew Shinkichi, who has a gambling problem.

Meanwhile, two Geishas, Okino (Yuko Daike) and Osei (Daigoro Tachibana) also roll into town. Siblings from the Naruto family seeking vengeance against the head of the Ginzo clan, the baddest clan of them all, for murdering their kin.

A third subplot involves a ronin, Hattori Genosuke played by superstar Tadanobu Asano. Hattori needs money to care for his sick wife Oshino (Yui Natsukawa) so he takes a job as a bodyguard/assassin for the Ginzo clan. His first assignment? Take out all the other clans. His actions set up a final showdown between Hattori and Ichi in the final act.

Regardless of the title, the focus of the film does not lie with Ichi, rather with the townspeople, the Geishas, and their combined struggles against the Ginzo clan. There's a lot of Kitano comedy to be found in these characters. Especially Shinkichi the large-faced gambling addict played by Taka Gadarukanaru (pronounced Guadalcanal) who is given center stage on several occasions.

First, he has a wonderful Three Stooges-esque encounter with some farmer boys wanting to learn swordsmanship. Then, during the gambling scenes and yet again, when he becomes fascinated with the Geisha Osei. Osei is a man living as a woman of exquisite beauty. Shinkichi's obsession becomes so great that he "borrows" Osei's makeup to make himself "more beautiful." It doesn't work.

There's also Aunty Oume's crazy neighbor (played by the single-monikered Muhomatsu) who runs circles around her house all day long, practically nude save for a helmet and mounted flag. The young man brandishes a spear and says nothing. He only screams as if charging into battle. Aunty Oume informs Ichi, "He thinks he's a Samurai." He is by far the most random and hilarious character in the film.

Speaking of random, there are also musical sequences. Long shots of farmers hoeing aren't just used to establish location. Their actions keep rhythm with the film's percussive soundtrack. It was the first time in 11 films that Kitano used a composer other than Joe Hisaishi and his collaboration here with *Keiichi Suzuki* is fabulous. The film concludes with the entire town gathering at the seasonal festival for an elaborate tap dance number with the modern dance troupe Stripes. Clearly a nod to Kitano's early days as a performer in Asakusa.

Along with his own history, Kitano also explores broader Japanese film history in his version of *Zatoichi*. Particularly in the long scene where Osei practices a dance routine to Shamisen accompaniment.

Early Japanese cinema often featured Geisha as their subjects. [1]Kitano features the dance rehearsal almost in its entirety, allowing Japanese and western audiences alike to absorb the intricacy of a traditional art form.

Overall, the film is entertaining, dynamic and different. 20 years on, Takeshi Kitano's *Zatoichi* serves as a template on how to reboot a beloved franchise the right way. It's a film that take chances and pulls no punches. What a shame he didn't make more!

TRAVEL AS AN EXPRESSION OF PERSONAL GROWTH AND IDENTITY IN SONATINE AND KIKUJIRO

The great thing about the films of Takeshi Kitano is that they work on many levels. Audiences can watch them to be entertained, and scholars can dig deeper. In his book, *Beat Takeshi vs. Takeshi Kitano*, author Casio Abe analyzes the films of Takeshi Kitano as having a symbolic meaning which serves to explore and resolve the inner conflict the artist has with his two public personas in his home country of Japan (Abe 1994.) One, a goofball comedian and the other, a serious actor and director.

Indeed, there are many examples of the search for personal identity present in Kitano's films. He often uses travel as a device through which his characters change and grow as the stories progress, even if the outcome of the journey is not a happy one.

Within *Sonatine* (1993), and *Kikujiro* (1999) we have two wonderful films that involve adult male characters whose behaviors regress in age as they travel from an urban environment to a rural one.

Using scholar Timothy Iles's theory of travel within film as a metaphor for "personal growth and understanding" as well as being representational of the stages of life itself (Iles 2008, 148), I will argue that both the act of travel and the resulting childlike behavior serves as a a function of Kitano's artistic exploration of his own personal identity.

There is no doubt that Kitano is an auteur. Because of the nature of the theory of auteurship, in which it is presumed that the chief creative force behind the film is creating a personal work of art,[1] the importance of Kitano's personal history (in particular his childhood and young adulthood) cannot be understated. Both *Sonatine* and *Kikujiro* contain autobiographical elements within them. Kitano himself has described the former as a "private film," (Gerow 2007, 102) and the title character in the latter is named after Kitano's father.

In *Sonatine*, Kitano plays Murakawa, a tired Yakuza who is sent by his boss to Okinawa with his cohorts to calm a feud with a rival gang. The movement of the group of men from the city to the rural begins with their arrival in Okinawa. We see a group shot of the men sitting on an airport shuttle bus in Naha. They resemble school boys seated geometrically as they would be on a field trip with blank, bored expressions.

When their Yakuza connection greets them, he goes so far as to offer them drinks and ice cream, looking very much like a school trip chaperone in his T-shirt and baseball cap. Symbolically, this is the beginning of the journey into the final stage of life for the men, which at once is signified by their representation as children.

This physical movement serves Iles's theory both spatially and temporally within the narrative of the film. First, the men are displaced from their familiar environment in the city of Tokyo. After a shootout in Naha, the survivors retreat to an isolated beach house. There, they are further rendered childlike in unfamiliar, rural surroundings with nothing to do.

The beach house serves as the primary location for a good chunk of the film's running time. Reviewer Tommy Udo points out "...one hour into the film, he just stops the plot and plays around for a while" (Udo 1999, 27.) It is at this point where the men engage in child's play on the beach, acting out Sumo tournaments and pretend gunfights with fireworks. In this location the men are free from the violence of their urban gangster lives. The two groups are in a holding pattern, waiting for something to happen between their superiors, free to play at their leisure on a beautiful, sun-soaked beach.

It should come as no surprise that it's Murakawa, a self-insert for Kitano, who acts as the "director" of the games. In the end, the two groups discover their mission is little more than a ruse to get them all out of town so the boss can increase his territory in Tokyo. Gang bosses aren't really known for their honesty.

The film's conclusion shifts locations from the beach house into a modern Naha hotel. It's not the urban sprawl of Tokyo, but nonetheless representative of a return to adulthood. The men engage in a shootout and Murakawa is left alone, the sole survivor. In a Hollywood film, he might walk off into the sunset, but this is Kitano's world. The images in Sonatine are Kitano's psyche made manifest. Murakawa sits in his car and shoots himself. It's bleak as Hell. Even if Murakawa returned to Tokyo, his boss would likely have him killed. The simplicity of life at the beach was his last look back at the innocence of childhood.

Similarly, the movement from urban to rural locations within the plot of *Kikujiro* (my favorite Kitano film) is symbolic of the personal journey of the protagonists as an extension of Kitano's own identity.

A young boy named Masao (Sekiguchi Yusuke) and an aging neighborhood gangster known only as "Mr." (Kitano) embark on a summer road trip to find the boy's biological mother whom Masao's grandmother says is "working away." At first, the incorrigible Mr. is only interested in the boy's travel money which he quickly loses gambling at the bicycle races. It isn't until later, when they become stranded in the countryside that Mr. begins to see the similarities between himself and the boy. It is only then he begins to take the journey seriously.

Along the way, they meet lots of interesting people and Masao receives the gift of a blue backpack adorned with a pair of white angel wings from a young couple who entertain him with juggling and dancing. When Masao puts on the backpack, he runs in circles, waving his arms as if in flight. It's the first time we see the boy smile. At the same time, we see the first instance of age regression by Kitano's character. As the shot widens, accompanied by Joe Hisaishi's unforgettable score, we see Mr. sitting on the grass, legs splayed like an infant, concentrating on learning how to juggle like the young lady.

The visuals announce that existing in a state of youthful rebellion brings happiness when the camera pans out to reveal a sign that reads, "Keep Off The Grass." This type of happiness cannot be found in Tokyo, where there is little grass, and arguably, no angels.

We see a similar shot in *Sonatine* when Ken (Terajima Susumu) is killed in front of Miyuki (Kokomai Aya) and Murakawa. Murakawa's infant-like posture on the beach is exactly the same as in *Kikujiro*. The difference is that *Sonatine* is about the end stages of Murakawa's life and the acceptance of death while *Kikujiro* is life-affirming. What changed between the two films? Kitano's motorcycle accident. At some point during his recovery, he went from exploring death on screen to embracing life in all its painful glory.

In his book, Casio Abe proposes that one way this cinematic stillness or death, is accomplished in *Sonatine* is through the use of expertly edited static shots of characters staring blankly, even in the presence of horrible events.

> Many of *Sonatine's* scenes begin with a silent, fully frontal medium shot of one of the participants in a developing situation. (In some cases, the sequence will also end with a formalized repetition of this initial shot.) Just as symmetry can be equated with death, the frontality of these scenes, which open with a medium shot, discreetly adds a slight shock of death to the movement on the screen (Abe, 1994, 109.)

Conversely, *Kikujiro* represents the earlier, more hopeful stages of life, as expressed by the lack of death and/or violence within the narrative as well as a greater number of tracking and moving shots. Despite being far lighter in content than *Sonatine*, life is not entirely devoid of difficulties in *Kikujiro*. In one scene, after being abandoned by Mr. in the park, Masao nearly becomes victim to a pedophile. It's probably the only time I've ever laughed while watching a scene dealing with such a repugnant subject. The scene weaves comedy and tragedy wonderfully.

Later, when Masao loses all hope of re-connecting with his biological mother, who has re-married and started a new family without consideration for her first-born, Mr. finally realizes that he and the boy have a lot in common.

As the plot progresses, the two characters begin to visually mirror one another. Masao takes on increasingly similar body language and mannerisms to that of Kitano, complete with twin trademark deadpan stoic expressions, limp arms dangling to the sides of his body and a distinctive lop-sided gate.

There are many shots where the man and the boy are posed identically, leaning on their arms, resting their faces in their hands. This characteristic body language is a trait that Takeshi developed during his Manzai years. Author Casio Abe describes "...his arms would almost always hang lifelessly by his side. By disassociating himself from "speaking with his hands," he ended up emphasizing his words" (Abe 1994, 12.) In this same manner, whenever a character in *Kikujiro* laughs or smiles, it has greater impact precisely because of the lack of physically expressed emotions throughout the majority of scenes. Rather than the stoic expressions being symbolic of death, here they are used to garner laughs once again drawing from Kitano's old days as a comedian.

When Masao reveals to Mr. that he has never even met his mother, Mr. exclaims to himself "So, he's just like me." The very next shot is a close-up of the angel wings on the backpack of Masao, which zooms out to a wide shot, revealing the man and boy walking side by side at an even pace, away from camera. On the cut, the music takes on a hopeful resonance, signifying that it is here, in this specific moment, their journey together truly begins within the narrative of the film.

Everything else that came before it serves as an introduction to their relationship, with distance being maintained through both the mechanisms of humor and drama, age difference, and most importantly, the selfishness of Mr., who, up until this point, is interested only in gambling, eating well and having fun. Not even the close encounter with the pedophile in the park, from which Mr. saves Masao, is enough to endear the boy to the man. It is not until Mr. discovers a shared parental history with his young companion, that he takes on the role of a true nurturer. In doing so, he serves to comfort both himself and the boy.

The film explores the emotional aspect of their journey together through their physical movement beginning with the scene at the bus stop. Their being "stuck" at the in this location for three days without transportation was only in their heads, announced by fact that that they eventually get up and walk.

When Mr. remarks "This bus stop must be 30 years old," and is then visited by his old Manzai partner Beat Kiyoshi, the location immediately takes on the metaphorical symbol of Kitano's personal past. It is therefore no surprise, that the two men exchange in quick banter that typified their successful Manzai act in the '70s and '80s. It is also while at the bus stop that Mr. finally masters juggling and tap dancing. Skills which also harken back to Kitano's days in Asakusa on stage as a comedian. The bus stop is perhaps an avatar for the France Theatre, where Kitano learned all the skills necessary to move on into his adult career as an entertainer away from his difficult childhood, as represented by Masao's life in the city. From this key point onward, Kitano ceases accompanying a little boy named Masao, but is metaphorically, accompanying a younger version of himself on a journey to understand his past.

As time passes in the film, the character of Mr. (and hence Kitano) becomes younger. He starts out as an adult in the city, and ends up as a child in the wilderness, playing with other "children." It is in this regression to childlike innocence that Mr. finds salvation, while at the same time, Masao is learning the hard lessons of growing up and gaining an understanding of what Iles calls "the less-than-innocent aspects of modern life" (Iles, 149.)

One visual that affirms this argument occurs after Masao finds out that mother has a new family and doesn't want him. Mr. runs off to find something to cheer him up. He returns with an angel bell. In a wide shot by the sea, we see an animation of Kitano's angel painting from the beginning of the film descend from the sky in the top of the frame. First, it hovers over Mr., and then moves down into Masao's area where it hovers over him briefly as well. Finally, it shrinks down, returning to inhabit the bell, which Masao is now ringing to summon a savior. The hovering pause by the angel over each character is symbolic that each is the savior of the other.

Later, after Mr. is beaten up by Yakuza for causing mischief at a local temple fair, Masao runs off in a similar fashion and retrieves bandages to dress his wounds and clean him up. Each character saves the other when the need arises.

Casio Abe confirms this analysis when he discusses the exchange of goods between the boy and Mr. as becoming more meaningful as the film progresses (Abe 1994, 244.) He points out that in the beginning, "Takeshi's yakuza only gives the child capitalist commodities such as a bicycle-racer outfit and a ten-thousand yen note" (ibid). Arguably, things found in an urban environment. But once they are out of the city and Kikujiro is closer to nature, and therefore himself, he gives the boy food, a makeshift hat crafted from a giant leaf, and the angel bell itself, which he tells the boy was left for him by his mother, and represents her love (ibid.)

Tying these ideas together and analyzing them for iconic content, Abe asserts that Takeshi is "waiting for the temporalization/mobilization of his own painting of an angel that appears during the title sequence" (Abe 1994, 243.) He also notes that it is the sound of the bell which initiates this motion (ibid), indicating Kitano's use of sound to complement his visuals.

Once they are in the wilderness, the film begins to take on a "camping" aspect. We see dragonflies, caterpillars, and butterflies amid the backdrop of the lush green, late summer locations. We now hear the constant hum of cicadas on the soundtrack. It is here where they become friends with the other "children" in the story and it's those relationships that make me love this film.

We have a travelling poet called "Mr. Nice Guy" and two bikers, "Fatso" and "Baldy." Together, the group sleeps outside, plays games, steals food from a local farm and behave like kids on summer vacation in the country away from the temptations and difficulties of city life, much in the same way the gangsters did in *Sonatine*. Again, we find Mr., played by Kitano, to be the director of the games in which he instructs the others in creative activities where they dress up in costumes to amuse the boy (and the man.)

The last 30 minutes of *Kikujiro* contrasts greatly with those of *Sonatine* in that Kitano finds salvation and renewal in the childlike behavior. At no point do the games become dark as they did in *Sonatine* with allusions of suicide or violence. There is no Russian Roulette here. This is the harmless mischief of eight-year-old boys, pure in heart and spirit.

Another place in which we find biographical significance to the life of Kitano is in the scene where Mr. decides to confront his own parental issues by riding a motorcycle to visit his mother in a nearby nursing home. It is significant that, after having transportation problems, he is driven to this important destination on the very vehicle on which he nearly died after crashing in 1994. In this key scene, Mr. observes his mother, an emotionally withdrawn, mentally ill woman. He does not approach or speak to her, but merely observes. Interestingly, Kitano's own mother passed away in 1999, the same year of *Kikujiro's* release.[2]

It is fitting that he is driven to the physical destination of his emotional epiphany by one of his "childlike" friends, Fatty. Up until this point, Mr. and Masao's journey has been repeatedly plagued with transportation problems. When Mr. tries to drive a stolen Taxi, it is revealed that he can't drive. Whichever cyclists at the racetrack he puts his money on fall down and crash. His attempts to get people to stop and pick them up along the roadside by placing nails in the road go awry, ending in a fight.

It is a popular trope of the "road movie" where characters encounter many problems getting from point A to point B, thus making the journey of personal discovery more difficult. Much like 1987's *Planes, Trains and Automobiles*, this plot device elongates the protagonist's journey, brings them into contact with all manner of interesting characters, and is the agency without which, the story would, ironically, not move forward. Kikujiro's inability to drive on his own as well as his being taken to his mother on the bike later, after having bonded with Masao, is also reflective, of Kitano's own resolution of emotional issues following his own near fatal motorcycle accident.

Laura Mulvey succinctly confirms this point when she quotes Gilles Deleuze in his writings on the 'movement-image' with "What counts is that the mobile camera is like a general equivalent of all the means of locomotion that it shows or that it makes use of – aeroplane, car, boat, bicycle, foot, metro..."

Also significant is the final scene in the woods before they return to Tokyo, where Mr., Masao and Mr. Nice Guy play a game of hide-and-seek with a barrel. When Masao finds Mr. and exclaims "Gotcha!" In this scene, Kitano, has in fact, found himself and can now return to civilization a changed man. When Mr.'s name is finally revealed back in Tokyo, it is that of Kitano's own father Kikujiro.

Iles sums it up:

> Thus, *Kikujiro no Natsu* offers an existential solution to the problem of alienation and urban isolation from tradition, from one's neighbours, and from one's self. This solution accepts the "motherless" condition of modern life- the isolation from tradition and from the natural world- and

proposes that nonetheless the individual may still draw compassionate support from his or her friends (the fellow travelers along the way) and may still arrive at a destination both important and profound (Iles, 2008, 149.)

Film scholars are certain to continue to focus on Kitano Takeshi as a subject of debate and analysis. Perhaps it is the blank, expressionless stare of this enigmatic talent that fascinates and begs for interpretation. Perhaps in the end, it is Kitano's stillness that takes on whatever traits we, the viewer, scholar or otherwise, ascribe to it. This opens the most interesting avenue of analysis of them all. That of the role of audience gaze. Without our stare, would Kitano's works have meaning?

Scholarly analysis aside, I like *Sonatine* for the way it pulls me into the story. I love *Kikujiro* for the warm and fuzzy feelings it gives me. No matter how many times I watch it, it always makes me smile.

PART TWO
KAIJU

"There's a little Godzilla in all of us."

YUJI SHINODA - *GODZILLA 2000*

ROARING INTO THE '90S

It's a universal truth going back all the way to 1910's *Frankenstein* that in movies there be monsters. Japan's history of making monster movies began in 1954 with Ishiro Honda's *Gojira*. The series, and others like it including Daiei Films' Gamera and Daimajin series are an important part of Japan's first golden age. They helped build Toho and Daiei into powerhouse studios.

The 1990s saw a revival of the kaiju film, when the technical side of the Japanese movie industry began to use CGI, with varying degrees of success.

Toho's Heisei series (named after the Heisei political era in Japan) began in 1984 with *The Return of Godzilla*, and ended during the second golden age in 1995 with the excellent *Gojira vs. Destroyah*. The Heisei *Rebirth of Mothra* trilogy targeted a younger more female demographic and ran from 1996 to 1998.

But it's Toho's competitor Daiei Film (later Kadokawa Daiei Studio) who comes out on top for the best kaiju films of this era. The reviews for the Gamera trilogy as well as others included in this section, originally appeared on BandSaboutmovies.com as part of their Kaiju Week series. They constitute what I consider to be the best kaiju films of the second golden age. Films that, while remaining suitable for younger viewers, approached the subject matter seriously, making them enjoyable for audiences of all ages.

At press time, there's a new animated Gamera reboot in the works from *Netflix* as well as more Godzilla entires slated to go into production. Giant monsters, whether friend or foe, never go out of style.

GAMERA: GUARDIAN OF THE UNIVERSE (1995)

In 1965, Daiei Studios decided to capitalize on Toho's successful Godzilla film series with their own fire-breathing radioactive star, Gamera the flying turtle. At that time, Gamera was "the friend to children." While critics generally regard the Gamera films from that era as largely inferior to the Toho productions, they are filled with creatively realized colorful sets and innovate quadrupedal monster designs, making them no less entertaining and fun then their larger-budgeted counterparts.

In 1995, after a 15-year retirement, Daiei brought back the shelled one and gave him a new lease on life. The man given the responsibility of transforming Gamera from a low-budget children's monster into a serious modern-day contender fell to director Shusuke Kaneko whose earlier work consists of several successful horror films and comedies. He did a great job.

In *Gamera: Guardian of the Universe*, we're give an updated origin story where Gamera was created by the ancient people of Atlantis who created him in response to the appearance of flocks of man-eating prehistoric birds called Gyaos - a favorite foe from the 1960's films.

The Japan Self -Defense Force misinterpret's Gamera's presence as a threat when his intentions are to save modern-day Japan from the birds. Only a few people understand his benevolent motives and they must convince the higher brass to put their military muscle behind the turtle.

Director Kaneko largely removes the element of young children and instead, opts to endow Gamera with a magical jewel that enables him to bond with a teenage girl on the brink of womanhood named Asagi (played by Steven Segal's daughter Ayako Fujitani.) Through Asagi, Gamera harnesses the added strength required to defeat the Gyaos in a grand battle that takes place entirely in broad daylight using only practical effects. Screw all the fancy CGI effects. This film is quite an ambitious undertaking for special effects director Shinji Higuchi whose shots blend seamlessly with Kankeo's.

Aside from the bigger budget retooling, the film also succeeds on a level far above that of the original series in the drama department. Kaneko treats the characters and plot with respect. There are no truly goofy moments in the subtitled version. More than any other director in the kaiju eiga genre, Shusuke Kaneko succeeds at melding humor and horror earnestly.

For those not into movies with guys in suits, *Gamera: Guardian of the Universe* succeeds on the same level as the "Rocky" films. Gamera gets beat up pretty badly early on, but comes back with fire-balls a-blazin' to kick some serious Gyaos tail feather.

This is one entertaining monster flick with as much ambition as you're ever going to see put into a movie of this kind. The sequels are even better, with the third in the trilogy *Gamera vs. Iris* (1999) considered by many to be the best kaiju film ever made. The Japanese language versions with English subtitles are definitely the way to go for all three of these films. Arrow Home Video's 2020 release of the entire Gamera collection featuring all the films from the first and second golden age on Blu Ray is amazing.

GAMERA 2: ATTACK OF LEGION (1996)
AKA GAMERA 2: THE ADVENT OF LEGION

1995's *Gamera: Guardian of the Universe* was a hit, prompting Daiei Film to produce the sequel, *Gamera: Attack of Legion* one year later. Ayako Fujitani returns as Asagi Kusanagi, the teen girl who enjoys a psychic bond with Gamera. The film also stars Japanese soap star Miki Mizuno. Miki comes from a line of kaiju eiga royalty. Her grandmother is Toho star Kumi Mizuno who appeared in no less than seven kaiju films. Miki plays a computer scientist who aids the military in unravelling the mysterious life cycle of earth's latest invader.

A far darker, scarier film than *Guardian*, this time, Gamera fights an alien from outer space called Legion. A symbiotic organism comprised of thousands of little one-eyed insect soldiers who unleash bloody attacks upon fully occupied trains and devour the electrical grid. Their mission is to prepare the earth for an intergalactic flower to grow. Electricity interferes with their ability to communicate with the collective and so anything electronic in their way has got to go.

Once mature, the space flower, will launch its seed with a destructive force equivalent to that of a thermonuclear device, propagating the species all over the world. There is also a queen Legion who, much to Gamera's dismay, sports shooting rays and tendrils as well as a nifty force field giving her the power to repel his fireballs.

The military fails in their attempts to assuage the Legion. It soon becomes evident that earth will become Legion's garden and the human race will cease to exist. The situation becomes even bleaker when Gamera is mortally wounded during an attempt to stop a seed from launching. It's one of the film's best special effects sequences set in the city of Sendai during the winter festival.

Our hero is literally left a mere shell of himself until he is revived by Asagi and a group of children who stand, hand-in-hand to endow him with their combined psychic strength. It's a nice way to acknowledge the children-focused '60s films while retaining a mature tone.

The end battle is astounding. The Suitmation and miniature cityscapes are superb. Shusuke Kaneko, Shinji Higuchi and crew have bested themselves ten-fold in creature design as well as in action sequences and drama. Gamera's design has evolved from the first film, taking on sea turtle characteristics while Legion is unlike any design that came before it.

During the suspenseful finale, the military finally decide to aid Gamera by distracting the Legion soldiers. Once this is accomplished, Gammy uses the life-force of the earth to boost his firepower to destroy the queen Legion. Mankind is once again safe but Asahi's jewel has shattered, breaking her psychic connection to Gamera permanently.

The final scene foreshadows darker things to come in the next film when one character asks, "But we wouldn't want Gamera as our enemy, would we?" No. No, we wouldn't. In the next film, we find out there are already people out there who regard him as a foe.

GAMERA 3: THE REVENGE OF IRIS (1999)
AKA GAMERA 3: THE AWAKENING OF IRIS

1995's *Gamera: Guardian of the Universe* was a considerably more adult film than its 1960s predecessors and was a hit with adults and youngsters alike, prompting the increasingly dark sequels *Gamera: The Advent of Legion* in 1996 and *Gamera 3: The Revenge of Iris* in 1999.

The first two films in the trilogy are very good. This movie is great. It's not just a monster movie, it's an art picture. It's the kaiju film that set a new standard in Japanese production. The genre film to compete with for all that came after.

In the first two installments of the trilogy (all written and directed by the very talented Shusuke Kaneko), Gamera derives his strength through his psychic link with a young teenage girl named Asagi played by Ayako Fujitani. In those films, he fights off invading monsters, including the giant bird-like reptilian Gyaos who prey on people like mice. No longer just a friend to children, Gamera is now an ancient guardian of humanity.

In this third installment, Gamera is a much darker deity. The people of Japan are sick of dealing with the destruction and unintended casualties from all our hero's battles. Our new heroine, 13-year-old Ayana (Ai Maeda) holds him personally responsible for the accidental death of her family three years earlier during a fight with Gyaos. Among the deceased is her beloved pet cat Iris. Rather than see Gamera as a saviour, she wants him dead.

When Ayana finds a large mysterious egg in a cave, she nurtures the ancient being and names it Iris. Kaneko deals with the theme of blossoming feminine maturity emerging in parallel with supernatural abilities overtly. Just as Asagi bonded with Gammy in the first two films, Ayana - a dark and brooding girl on the brink of womanhood - psychically bonds with the new villain. The new monster Iris absorbs and integrates Ayana's malice for Gamera fully and grows into maturity simultaneously with Ayana. When Iris enters adolescence, she brutally attacks Gamera.

At the film's climax, Iris physically absorbs Ayana's entire body in a marvelous sequence of soft dissolves. The soundtrack cuts to a single heartbeat. Ayana floats in the fetal position inside Iris amongst amniotic fluid. The amazingly hypnotic scene concludes with the critically wounded Gamera rising to rescue her by ripping into Iris's womb. He gets his right arm blown off in the process, proving once and for all to Ayana that he is the benevolent kaiju we've all come to know and love. She just couldn't see it.

Realizing the error of her ways, Ayana thanks Gammy in a quiet moment as emotionally effective as any between Fay Wray and King Kong. Just then, a massive flock of Gyaos approaches the city. Gamera's strength is depleted and he's close to death. Nonetheless, our weary hero marches off to fight for mankind – probably for the last time.

Fortunately for us, Gamera is one in a long line of guardian deities created by the forward-thinking Atlantians of old, leaving the possibility for further entries in the series. Sadly, this would be the final time Kaneko would direct a Gamera movie. But it would not be his last time at the helm of a kaiju eiga.

Gamera 3 uses the tried-and-true Suitmation/miniature model methods of classic kaiju special effects in combination with '90s CGI to admirable results. Although few and far between, every action sequence is thrilling. The plot and characters are interesting. The film's only deficiency lies in an underdeveloped sub-plot involving a mystical doomsday cult that worships Iris and attempts to wrangle control of the beast from Ayana.

When the credits to this film rolled at the American premiere at the Egyptian Theatre in Los Angeles in 1999, the audience awarded Kaneko-san with a five-minute standing ovation. When the lights came up, he stood up, a few rows in front of me, turned toward the audience and bowed. He took in the love, with his hand on his heart and his face filled with emotion. Many people think Japanese giant monster movies are silly. If any film can change that viewpoint, it's this one.

GODZILLA 2000 (1999)
AKA GODZILLA MILLENNIUM

Godzilla 2000 was the first attempt to reboot the beloved film series for a new audience since 1995's *Godzilla vs. Destroyah*. Directed by Takao Okawara, the film abandons the story line of all of its predecessors save for the original 1954 film. Shinoda (Takehiro Murata) and his daughter Io (Mayu Suzuki) run a G network of scientists trying to learn all they can about Godzilla and his enormous regenerative abilities. A newspaper reporter named Yuki (Naomi Nishida) accompanies them.

Katagiri (played by a glowering Hiroshi Abe) works for the government and believes that Godzilla should be killed for the protection of humanity.

While Shinoda's group gathers information on the big guy, Katagiri's group accidentally awakens an alien dubbed Orga, who has been slumbering beneath the sea since prehistoric times when it crash landed on earth. It wakes up when inadvertently exposed to sunlight during an exploratory undersea expedition meant to search for new energy resources for Japan.

Once it has gained enough strength, Orga rises from the sea, first as a shiny CGI alien craft. After soaking up some more power from the sun, it morphs into several interesting forms, one of which resembles a silver manta ray. Orga attempts to permanently adapt to earth's atmosphere by sampling Godzilla's "Regenerator G-1" healing cells in order to clone him. This naturally upsets Godzilla and predictably, the flames fly.

While an enjoyable film on many levels, it's visually uneven. Many of the daylight effects shots expose poor blue screen and ineffective CGI integration.

The finale is the best reason to watch the film. The night battle is much more effective (mostly because they don't use a lot of CGI) and the climactic showdown between the final form of the alien Orga and 'Zilla utilizes both excellent miniatures and pyrotechnics.

The film's kaiju designs are a big success. This manifestation of the big guy quickly became a fan favorite and is still my favorite today. He has a sleeker, more muscular torso, longer purple dorsal spines and pugnacious visage which more than adequately conveys his strength and personality. He is intelligent and tenacious, easily riled and loves to have the last roar, as evidenced by his gloating display following the defeat of Orga. For fans of Godzilla, it is a very satisfying conclusion.

This was the first time an American studio gave a Godzilla film a wide U.S. theatrical release since *Godzilla 1985* and it is probably the only case in history where the American version surpasses the Japanese. The U.S. version benefits from additional sound effects and foley to fill in the dead air of the original's soundtrack. It trims the sluggish plot and even handles the English language dubbing with more respect than its predecessors up to that time, despite the occasional addition of corny dialogue like, "Eeehh, quit your bitching!" In this case, seeking out the American version is definitely the preferred choice. It's my favorite Godzilla film from the second golden age.

GODZILLA, MOTHRA, KING GHIDORAH: GIANT MONSTERS ALL-OUT ATTACK (2001)
AKA GMK

GMK is not a particularly great film or even one of my favorites. I'm including this review for two reasons. First, it was probably the most anticipated kaiju film to come out during the second golden age. Expectations were high for *GMK* and the film's director, Shusuke Kaneko, who redefined the kaiju genre with his Heisei Gamera trilogy. Second, it's the first Godzilla film to overtly explore Japan's role in World War II in almost 50 years.

GMK wipes the slate clean yet again and starts another entirely new time line in the G universe, as a direct sequel to the original *Gojira*.

Godzilla has not been seen since 1954 when Dr. Serazawa killed him using The Oxygen Destroyer. Recently, the wreckage of a submarine was discovered off the coast of Guam and General Tachibana (Ryudo Uzaki) of the Japanese Self-Defense Force is starting to suspect that Godzilla is responsible.

Tachibana's daughter Yuri (Chiharu Nîyama), with whom the general has a strained relationship, works for a reality TV show called Digital Q. The show specializes in stories on myths and cryptids like the Blair Witch and Bigfoot. In other words, legends containing a lot of fictional details meant to boost ratings. That is, until Yuri and her crew stumble upon the real thing.

They meet a mysterious old professor played by Toho kaiju movie veteran Eisei (Hideyo) Amamoto (Dr. Hu from *King Kong Escapes*) named Isayama The Prophet. The old man tells Yuri that Godzilla will soon return to exact terrible retribution against Japan for all of the horrors the country perpetrated during World War II. He claims that while there are no manmade weapons strong enough to fight Godzilla, if the three Guardian Monsters - Mothra, Baragon, and King Ghidorah - are awakened, perhaps they can work together to stop him.

There are no clever metaphors here. It's explicitly stated that Godzilla is comprised of all the souls of those who died in the war. He's not the good guy anymore. He's a kaiju filled with thousands of onryo, a traditional type of ghost believed to be capable of harming the living, injuring or killing enemies, or even causing natural disasters. Typically, an onryo (like Sadako from *Ringu*) exacts revenge to "redress" the wrongs it received while it was alive. Remember all those young pilots who were fed speed and forced to go on kamikaze missions? Well, they're back and they're inside the meanest Godzilla ever.

After encountering Baragon burrowing a tunnel, Yuri's goal becomes to report the kaiju story as accurately as possible at any cost. Simultaneously, her father is trying to destroy Godzilla.

While visually excellent, *GMK* does not entirely live up to expectations in some areas.

In the *Gamera* series, Kaneko was often criticized for having too much story and not enough monster action. This film suffers from the exact opposite malady. You may wonder, "Does story really matter in a giant monster movie?" Probably not. The fights are staged very well with lots of nods and winks to best kaiju battles of the past 50 years.

The special effects and suit designs are some of the best ever with the final battle between Mothra, Godzilla and King Ghidorah being particularly ambitious. The daylight stand-off between Baragon and Godzilla was pleasantly reminiscent of the work of Ishiro Honda in such '60s films as *Monster Zero* and *Destroy All*

Monsters. I loved the fact that Kaneko included Baragon, who hadn't appeared in a film since 1968. Fan service done right.

The biggest disappointment is the musical score by Kaneko regular Ko Otani. There are a few good cues (such as the theme when adult Mothra breaks forth from her cocoon) but most of it strays a little too deep into John Barry territory to establish its own identity. The classic theme by Akira Ifukube is only used once at the very end of the film, albeit to great effect.

Is *GMK* a better production than its predecessors *Godzilla 2000* and *Godzilla vs. Megaguirus*? You bet it is. The American reboot *Godzilla* (2014) with Bryan Cranston and its sequels owe a lot to this film in terms of story. What a shame Kaneko wasn't brought on board for those. I'd love to see a Japanese director try to make a kaiju film in Hollywood. Better yet, a kaiju film produced in Japan bankrolled by a U.S. studio with big money and promotion behind it. Wouldn't that be something?

———

PART THREE
J-HORROR

"All the things that used to be inside of me... now they are all outside."

MAMIYA - *CURE*

CUTTING ACROSS CULTURES AND MEDIUMS

The J-horror boom of the 1990s cannot be understated in terms of its importance to there being a second golden age of Japanese cult cinema. The '90s saw the release of many Japanese horror films in the west both on DVD and theatrically in larger cities. Rather than dubbing the films, most were released with subtitles. Despite positive and critical and audience reception of the Japanese versions, Hollywood bought up a few of these properties and remade them with American actors.

The Ring (2002), directed by Gore Verbinski made only minor changes to the story from the original *Ringu* (1998) and was a huge success. *The Grudge* (2004) and its sequel were both helmed by the original's Japanese director Takashi Shimizu at the behest of producer Sam Raimi. *Dark Water* (2005) wasn't the last J-Horror remake but it is the final to fall within the time frame covered within this book.

Not only were these remakes good, but they proved that Japanese ghost stories translate well for audiences outside Japan. The *Ringu* franchise in particular, has crossed not only borders, but mediums, having started out as a series of successful books written by Koji Suzuki.

The first adaptation came in the form of a Japanese television series in 1995. The Japanese film series began in 1999 and the Hollywood remake came out in the early 2000s. The entire project came full circle when the books were translated into English and released in North America. While most film journalists and scholars concentrate on the changes between the Japanese films and their American counterparts, I went back and read the books. The resulting comparison essay is included here.

Another J-horror filmmaker who gained notoriety during the second golden age is Takashi Miike. His film *Audition* is taught in films schools today. But it's his contribution to the Asian anthology film *Three Extremes* (2004) and the horror musical/comedy *The Happiness of the Katakuris* (2001) that I find most interesting.

Also in this section is an analysis of the film that started it all for me, *Cure* by Kiyoshi Kurosawa. It is not only my favorite film from this era, it's the one that sent me down the rabbit hole of learning all I could about Japanese cult cinema I discussed in the introduction. The films he has directed outside of the second golden age continue to entertain, win awards and invite analysis.

What I love about him the most is his ability to create films that might be interpreted through a diverse array of lenses in various ways. Viewers will inevitably walk away from a Kiyoshi

Kurosawa film with questions and there are no correct or incorrect answers. For me, his films have a hypnotizing effect. Just like Mesmer in *Cure*, "the other" Kurosawa has the ability to put audiences into a trance. It is for that reason, I've chosen to close this book with a look at the symbolism in *Cure*.

LOST IN ADAPTATION
RINGU FROM NOVEL TO SCREEN

Beginning in the late 1990s, Japanese Horror cinema, by this time known as J-horror, experienced an extremely creative and financially successful period. Chief among these films responsible for the boom was Nakata Hideo's *Ringu* (1998), based on the Suzuki Koji novel of the same name.

The story concerns a reporter named Asakawa who faces a race against the clock to break the curse of a videotape of unknown origin that kills everyone who watches it in seven days. The tape contains a collage of disjointed but disturbing images that serve as puzzle pieces to the mystery. While attempting to find a way to break the spell, Asakawa uncovers the mystery of the woman behind the tape, the seemingly unappeasable vengeful intersex spirit of one Sadako Yamamura.

The plot thickens after Reiko watches the tape, receives a phone call announcing that she too will die and then accidentally leaves the tape out for her young son to watch. The clock is now ticking. Reiko is stressed to the point where she enlists the aid of her estranged husband. Unfortunately he also watches the tape and now the ex couple must solve the puzzle before the seven days are up.

With three protagonists in jeopardy, the movie takes on an

urgency that builds slowly in intensity. The videotape includes the image of a girl brushing her hair in front of a mirror and a static shot of a well. These things are not scary in and of themselves, but they're cut together in such an odd way, they feel unsettling.

Instead of leaving the viewer feeling satisfied as each little clip of the video tape's meaning is revealed, the viewer feels more and more uneasy. Each time, we the audience, see just enough to get our imaginations going. It's a film that hands over no explanations on a silver platter.

In the end, the only way to survive is to copy the tape and pass it along for someone else to watch, thus propagating the curse infinitely, kind of like an old-fashioned chain letter.

Since the film's release and the subsequent American re-make *The Ring* in 2002, much has been written in the way of scholarly analysis related to the original Japanese production.

In his article *The Original and the Copy: Nakata Hideo's Ring* (1998), author Julian Stringer points out that there has been little to no scholarly attention paid to Suzuki's original novel and the role it has played in relation to the films (Stringer 2007, 302-303). Indeed, the differences between the books and the films are frequent and varied.

Among the most interesting changes are those related to issues of gender and sexuality. Most of the English language work in the area of feminist film theory has been related to American or European horror cinema with the J-horror phenomena being largely overlooked in favor of a broader framework of cultural discourse (Blake 2007; White 2005; Stringer 1998.)

By combining these two ideas and focusing on the 1991 novel and the 1998 film, it is possible to apply feminist film theory to both and compare their meanings. Although the film changes many elements related to gender and sexuality from the novel, each version adheres to the feminist film theory of authors Barbara Creed, Carol J. Clover, and others (Creed 1993; Clover 1992; Doherty 2005; Williams 1996.) Furthermore, the question as to why these changes were made in the transition from book to film will be postulated.

The film differs from the novel in several important ways. First, the protagonist Asakawa changes from a married man with an infant daughter to a divorced, working mother raising a seven-year-old clairvoyant son on her own. Second, the character of Ryuji is changed from a cynical, unlikeable, self-proclaimed rapist to the sullen but brilliant ex-husband of Asakawa, who, like his son, is psychically empowered. Third and most importantly, ghost Sadako Yamamura changes from an intersex rape victim into an asexual hybrid human monster.

In changing the protagonist from male newspaper reporter Kazuyuki Asakawa, to female Television reporter Reiko Asakawa, *Ringu* serves several functions within the maternal component of feminist film theory.

Exchanging Kazuyuki for Reiko (played by Matsushima Nanako) brings forth maternal issues not present in the novel and reminiscent of what author Thomas Doherty refers to as Sigourney Weaver's awakening maternal instincts in the film *Aliens* (1986) (Doherty 2005, 195.) In that film, Weaver's character Ripley overcomes the loss of her child (a fact only revealed in the director's cut of the film) through her "adoption" of the little girl Newt.

In *Ringu,* Reiko overcomes the emotional loss of her son, who is growing distant by the day, through her act of maternal love towards Sadako at the end of the film. In both cases the women lost their biological children because of their jobs. Ripley because she was stranded in space for 57 years at the end of the first *Alien* (1979) where she was doing her job aboard the spaceship Nostromo. Reiko because of her focus and dedication to her job at the TV station. The only difference is that Ripley's loss is physical while Reiko's is emotional.

Spatially, Reiko's descent into the damp tunnel of the well at the end of *Ringu* and the subsequent ascent of Sadako's remains from the fluid to be embraced lovingly by Reiko are visually parallel to Doherty's assertion that Ripley's search for Newt in *Aliens* (1986) amid the maze of the Queen's alien's moist, hot lair is "a night-sea journey that reenacts the passage through the birth canal" (Doherty 2005, 195.) Interestingly, in both cases, the women act more as mid-wife or adoptive mother to the child in question, with Ripley gently lifting Newt from the alien's captive alien egg sack and Reiko lifting Sadako from the bottom of the well.

Reiko's difficult relationship with her son Yoichi is compounded by the fact that he is different from other children. He possesses clairvoyant abilities and is quiet and serious in his mannerisms. He's almost an adult in a child's body.

In his first scene in the film, it is established that Yoichi and his mother have reversed roles in their two-person family unit. He readies her clothes for her to attend the funeral of his cousin Tomoko, who died after watching the video with friends in a woodland cabin. He even helps Reiko zip the back of her dress.

With the absence of a male presence in the house, Yoichi has stepped into that role. Certainly, the scene where Reiko catches Yoichi watching the cursed tape is indicative of her inability to protect him in a traditionally maternal fashion.

In the novel, Kazuyuki Asakawa rarely helps his wife with their daughter Yoko. He is entirely focused on his job. In this case, however, it is without any great loss to his relationship with the child . He and his wife are happily married. Each character fulfills their classic Japanese gender specific roles in the home. It is only the female version of Asakawa, Reiko, who suffers in her relationship with her child when she focuses on her career.

Although Asakawa's change from male in the novel to female in the film might appear outwardly to be progressive, both *Ringu* the book and the movie effectively espouse the benefit of the traditional gender roles in each version. It begs the question as to why this change was made in the adaptation process.

Author Linda Williams asserts that in the horror genre, we often see female protagonists face dire consequences because of their gaze, which serves to identify them with the monster they are facing against the backdrop of a male dominated world (Williams 1996, 18.)

If we apply this theory to Nakata's *Ringu*, we find that indeed, Reiko's trouble begins after she watches the videotape and that she and Sadako (the monster) have much in common. First, both Reiko and Sadako are dealing with supernatural powers within the family dynamic. Reiko has an ex-husband and a son who are psychically endowed. Sadako and her mother Shizuko dealt with the same issue during their lives.

Second, Reiko works for the media, with her career causing tensions with her husband. The deviation from her perceived acceptable gender role leads to their separation. Reiko's media job destroys her marriage. Similarly, the media destroys the Yamamura family unit when they turn on Sadako's mother Shizuko and accuse her of being a fraud rather than a true psychic.

Ironically, the only reason Shizuko went public with her abilities in the first place is because she was convinced to do so by a male named Dr. Ikuma, who financially supports the Yamamuras and attempts to publicly exploit Shizuko's abilities in order to further his own career.

Another reason for the change in the protagonists gender might be because young males, who comprise the main demographic of horror film audiences around the globe[1] are perhaps more inclined to sympathize with a female protagonist in distress than a male one (Clover 1992, 5.)

> Author Carol J. Clover asserts, "male viewers are quite prepared to identify not just with females, but with females in the horror-film world…screen females in fear and pain" (Clover 1992, 5.)

It is important to note that it is in the *Ringu* novel that the male Asakawa identifies with Sadako Yamamura via the visual medium of the cursed videotape. Rather than existing within the context of a male dominated society, as Reiko in the film does,

Asakawa effectively becomes the male viewer of a horror film within the novel. This element helps to create a self-aware intertextual work much more complex than the film version.

Clover argues that in film, audience-character identification is often most successfully achieved via handle-held, first person point-of-view shots (Clover 1992, 8.) However, it is only in the novel that the cursed video is represented this way. Especially when Asakawa watches it for the first time. The text establishes this feat in cinematic terms, even using the words camera and shot in the passage:

> This was clearly a volcanic eruption, a natural phenomenon, a scene that could be explained. The molten lava flowing from the mouth of the volcano threaded its way down through ravines and headed this way. Where was the camera positioned? Unless it was an aerial shot, it looked like the camera was about to be swallowed up (Suzuki 2007, 90.)

Also in the novel, Asakawa is placed into the head of Sadako at the point in the tape when the people who tormented her in life begin to flash onscreen. He is, in effect, seeing Sadako's memories as she experienced them, filtered by her point of view in the following excerpt:

> By now there were perhaps a thousand faces: they had become nothing but black particles, filling the screen until it looked like the television had been turned off, but the voices continued. It was more than Asakawa could bear. All that criticism, directed right at him. That's how it felt (Suzuki 2007, 92.)

The author's use of the word "felt" in this instance brings into focus the difference between a reader's engagements with the medium of literature versus an audience's gaze while watching a film. Although an attempt is made in the film to create the characters' emotional submersion into the tape via matching eye level shots, we (the audience) are removed from their gaze through the cross cutting to their reactions and instead, are left to watch them watching the video. In the novel, words like "felt" and other adjectives serve to force the reader to identify with the subject in the book. We "see" the video through Asakawa's eyes who sees it through Sadako's.

It is at this point in the novel when a baby appears on the cursed video and Asakawa is put in the place of the feminine, indeed, the mother, adding another layer of psychosexual complexity to the proceedings. Once again, the aim is achieved via a cinematic style of writing. Was this riveting part of the novel the inspiration for the filmmakers to change Asakawa from a male to a female in the adaptation process? Nakata has never been on the record as saying so.

But Creed's argument for a fluid notion of identification between audience, victim and monster[2] can be applied to both versions of *Ringu*, specifically in terms of Sadako's "mothering and reproductive functions" (Creed 1993, 7, 155.) It is never clearer than in the passage:

On-screen, he could now see hands holding the baby. The left hand was under its head, and the right was behind its back, holding it carefully. They were beautiful hands. Totally absorbed by the image, Asakawa found himself holding his own hands in the same position. He heard the birth cry directly below his own chin. Startled, he pulled back his hands. He had felt something. Something warm and wet - like amniotic fluid, or blood - and the weight of flesh. Asakawa jerked his hands apart, as if casting something aside, and brought his palms close to his face. A smell lingered. The faint smell of blood - had it come from the womb, or...? His hands felt wet. But in reality, they weren't even damp. He restored his gaze to the screen. (Suzuki 2007, 91.)

Sadako's desire to have children despite her inability to do so) is removed completely from the film version of *Ringu*. It is featured prominently in the novel. She is intersex, possessing the genitalia of box sexes but has no uterus. When she visits Ryuji at the appointed time of his death, he ponders the previously described scene in his head in the selection:

> What did Sadako give birth to? The hint was right here, so close at hand. He hadn't realized that Sadako's power had become fused with another power. She'd wanted to have a child but her body couldn't bear one. So, she'd made a bargain with the devil – for lots of children (Suzuki 2007, 264.)

Curiously, Ryuji, who is possibly the most interesting character in the novel, is not frightened of Sadako Yamamura's curse throughout most of the narrative. The more he learns about her, the more his fascination grows. He is seduced by her. It is only at the exact moment of his death that he fears her. His last thought is that of her reproductive cycle, once again placing the subtext within the scope of Creed's maternal theory (Creed 1993, 155). Ryuji poses the question to Asakawa in the dialogue:

> Male and Female? It used to be that all living things were hermaphroditic like worms or slugs with both female and male sex organs. Don't you think that's the ultimate symbol of power and beauty (Suzuki 2007, 213?)

Author Suzuki's choice to give the character of Ryuji the greatest understanding of Sadako is an interesting one, given that Ryuji is a man who claims to have raped at least three different women in his lifetime (Suzuki 2007, 91.)

He holds a disdainful outlook towards people and life in general and is coded masculine in every sense of the word. He is described as athletic, with angular features. When asked by Asakawa about his dreams for the future, Ryuji responds casually with "While viewing the extinction of the human race, I would dig a hole in the earth and ejaculate into it over and over again" (Suzuki 2007, 91.)

Ryuji's fantasy is to literally create a vagina in mother earth and violate her repeatedly, degrading her with his semen in an act that would not produce children in the traditional sense. Only a truly twisted mind like his could possibly understand the rage and torment Sadako's spirit suffers.

Author Leticia Glocer Fiorini supports this theory when she explores Freud's theory that "the mother is always present in a man: first at his origin; then in the woman he loves, chosen for her similarity to his mother; and finally when he returns to Mother Earth" (Fiorini, 2010, 89.)

But, despite being unlikeable, Ryuji is much more level-headed than Asakawa and is frequently characterized as being both physically and emotionally stronger than his friend. Asakawa actually admires him to some degree, seeing him as fearless, eloquent and decisive (Suzuki 2007, 243-244.)

Most importantly, it is Ryuji's firsthand understanding of the mind of a rapist that allows him to ferret out Dr. Nagao's (the novel's version of Dr. Ikuma) past violation and murder of Sadako (Suzuki 2007, 220), thus uncovering the key reason for why she has returned from the grave to take revenge on the living.

In the film, the issue of Ryuji being a rapist is removed. Instead, he is given the role of Reiko Asakawa's ex-husband. Not coincidentally, he is also an absentee father to their son, Yoichi. This change creates a narrative parallel between Yoichi and Sadako. Both children have supernatural abilities in life and both are the children of single mothers.

Rather than portraying Ryuji's otherness through his hatred of mankind (which helps him to understand an outsider like

Sadako) the motion picture Ryuiji's otherness is represented in the form of psychic abilities similar to those of Sadako's mother, Shizuko.

As in the novel, he uses this instinct at the same point in story to discover the injustice done to Sadako, this time by Dr. Ikuma, who does not rape her, but murders her and throws her into the well just the same.[3]

Rape is one of the key facets of the novel that is entirely removed from the film version of *Ringu*. This change removes much of Sadako Yamamura's status as victim. Thus, the reasons for revenge lose some of their impact, necessitating the need for a device to render her more frightening.

The film achieves this by changing her into a literal monster, half human and half sea demon. This is surmised in the scene describing Sadako's mother Shizuko sitting for hours watching the sea (for her lover?) and also by the repeated phrase "Frolic in brine, goblins be thine."

Sadako's de-humanization is achieved visually in the film as well. In the novel, she is described as possessing a great delicate beauty by her rapist, Dr. Nagao. In the film, we never see her face. Even in the scenes where she is shown in flashbacks before her death, her long, black hair completely covers her face. Her posture is hunched and her movements jerky, creating an air of unnatural freakishness. This manifestation of hybrid monster helps to remove the empathy that the reader feels towards Sadako and renders her an instrument of evil up until the scene in the well where Reiko cradles her remains as a mother cradles a child.

It is the Dr. in the book who comes across as inhuman, rather than Sadako as he coldly describes her rape in lieu of discovering that she is intersex as "a necessary trial if she were to go on living as a woman."

He is further shown to be calculating and cruel. Along with raping Sadako, he exploits Sadako's mother's Shizuko's mental gifts for financial gain. After receiving a telepathic death threat from Sadako, who is arguably enraged over being attacked, Nagao panics and decides to kill her.

The inner conflict he feels at having not only committed rape, but also having done so to a beautiful woman with male genitalia is quite clear in the dialogue when he says, "On the one hand, I desired the destruction of her body, but on the other hand, I didn't want her body to be marred." He desires her, but he also fears for the loss of his own masculine identity from having raped an intersex person.

The novel contains conventions within the rape-revenge subgenre of horror films explored by Clover and other scholars.

Certainly, Sadako's treatment in the film gives her sufficient cause for her posthumous revenge. She was after all, killed and thrown down a well. But the inclusion of rape was perhaps too much for the aforementioned predominantly young male audience with a fluid notion of identification between audience, victim and monster.

Clover further substantiates this point when she questions what affect the identification of a rapist might have on a male audience in the following passage:

> The male viewer's stake might be in imagining himself reacting to that most quintessentially feminine of experiences. The answer lies, perhaps, in the question: is it precisely *because* rape is the most quintessentially feminine of experiences - the limit case of powerlessness and degradation - that it is such a powerful motivation, such a clean ticket, for revenge? (Clover, 154.)

Indeed, there is a moment in the novel where Dr. Nagao forces the reader to imagine what it must have been like being Sadako during her violation. "What did my face look like then? What did she see when she looked at me? The face of a beast, I'm sure. That's what I was thinking as I finished" (Suzuki 2007, 223.)

In the novel, the cursed video contains this very image, once again forcing our male protagonist Asakawa to experience the feminine. He feels her rape as he watches the tape just as he experienced giving birth earlier in the video.

Clover cites author Marco Starr in regards to the phenomenon of the "woman-identified" man with regards to perhaps the most notorious rape-revenge film of them all, *I Spit On Your Grave* (1977) (Clover 118-119.) In the discussion, the fact that men were uncomfortable watching the film gets to the heart of why it is likely that the filmmakers of *Ringu* (1998) who are male, dropped the subject of rape during the adaptation process. Clover cites Starr's following explanation:

> Watching a film as personally intense as *I Spit on Your Grave* is, to some degree, an upsetting experience under any circumstances. To watch it in the presence of a large, mostly male audience, however, is to witness the film with some terrified viewers, despite appearances to the contrary. The realization that one's fellow viewers are potential rapists can be devastating when one is relating to the experience of being raped (Clover 1992, 119.)

I Spit On Your Grave (1977) has much in common with *Ringu* the novel. First, each depicts rape in very much the same way in regards to the perpetrator's attitude toward the victim. Dr. Nagao defends himself by not only describing Sadako's great beauty, but it is later justified a second time by Ryuji who theorizes that Nagao was forced into it by Sadako herself, in a bid to lose her virginity before committing suicide at Nagao's hands (Suzuki 231-232.).

Ryuji, who is a rapist himself, is essentially saying that Sadako asked for it in the same manner that Johnny and the other men accuse Jennifer Hills (played by Camille Keaton) of "wanting it" just because she is wearing shorts on a hot summer day in *I Spit On Your Grave*.

The discomfort felt by male audiences in regards to the issue of rape is probably best summarized by male author Matt Hills when he observed that the *Ringu* novel is "far more uncomfortable in its representations of gender and sexuality than both the Japanese and American film adaptations" (Hills 2005, 162.)

But it is Sadako's inability to reproduce in the traditional way that gives both the novel and the film credence to Creed's maternal theories (Creed 1993, 166.) As an intersex individual in the novel, she has no uterus and can therefore not bare children. Nonetheless, it is through the sex act with Dr. Nagao (who has the smallpox virus at the time of the rape) that Sadako becomes able to reproduce herself when her supernatural abilities combine with the virus and create otherworldly offspring of ceaseless regeneration (Suzuki 2007.)

In her own way, Sadako is mating with everyone who watches the cursed tape. The act of reproducing the videotape allows the cursed viewers to survive.

Without reproduction, the viewers die a horrible death through Sadako's stare. It brings to mind Creed's use of the phrase "The Medusa's Gaze" (166), which draws immediate parallels between the myth of Medusa and the myth of Sadako Yamamura in *Ringu*.

When Perseus slew the Medusa he did not – as commonly thought – put an end to her reign or destroy her terrifying powers. Afterwards, Athena embossed her shield with the Medusa's head. The writhing snakes, with their fanged, gaping mouths, and the Medusa's own enormous teeth and lolling tongue were on full view. Athena's aim was simply to strike terror into the hearts of men as well as remind them of their symbolic debt to the imaginary castrating mother. No doubt she knew what she was doing. After all, Athena was the great Mother-Goddess of the ancient world and according to ancient legend, the daughter of Metis, the goddess of wisdom, also known as the Medusa (166.)

Like Medusa as described by Creed (Creed, 1993, 166), Sadako is not vanquished at the end of the film, but continues on and on through the video, which must be reproduced to break the curse.

Anyone who watches the tape and figures out the secret to survival becomes one of Sadako's children in the same way that Athena propagated the myth of Medusa, her mother. It is perhaps appropriate that both the *Ringu* novels and films have propagated the world over.

The differences with regards to gender and sexuality between *Ringu* the novel and the movie *Ringu* (1998) each has its own distinct meaning despite the changes made in the adaptation process from book to film, As we have seen, each can be analyzed via the concepts in feminist film theory explored by scholars Carol J. Clover, Barbara Creed, Thomas Doherty and more (Creed 1993; Clover 1992; Doherty 2005; Williams 1996.)

Nakata's adaptation of the novel highlights an ongoing Japanese adherence to a doctrine of separate spheres of activity for the sexes, whereby women's biological destiny is to nurture the next generation and not compete with men within the job market, Reiko embodies the plight of the ambitious Japanese woman who is also a mother, whilst Sadako becomes the thwarted potentiality of all victims of masculine aggression" (Blake 2007, 217-218.)

Future scholarly analyses might postulate how gender roles in the nation of Japan changed after the nation's defeat in World War II when the U.S. began to influence Japanese Government policy and culture. Author Jay McRoy brings up this very question in relation to the creation of Japan's Constitution in 1946 (McRoy 2008, 79) which he argues, changed everything for men and women in the following passage:

> This post war text has had an extensive impact upon gender roles in contemporary Japan, reconfiguring the multiple ways in which the nation's populace imagines the sex and gender-based apportioning of social and cultural roles, as well as the impact of conventional and emerging conceptions of masculinity and femininity (McRoy 2008, 79.)

Whatever the future holds for the scholarly discussion on the *Ringu* series of films and books, it is certain that the research and debate will rage on. The series has proved popular both in its home country of Japan as well as in the west, where Gore Verbinski's American remake *The Ring* was hugely successful, spawning a sequel during the second golden age.

The tale of Sadako Yamamura has proliferated in a variety of mediums all around the world. It is perhaps a fact that would please Sadako herself. Her legend (i.e. her progeny) goes on and on and on, not only in the novels and films themselves but in the research and exploration of those works.

RINGU 2 (1999)

Ringu 2, released only one year after the smash hit original, picks up where the first film left off. We are introduced to a new character named Takano Mai (Miki Nakatani), a psychic who is investigating the cursed videotape which kills anyone who watches it seven days later. In particular, she is curious about the involvement of her recently deceased boyfriend, Professor Ryuji Takayama (Hiroyuki Sanada) from the first film.

The leads are few and far between as Ryuji's ex-wfie Reiko and their son Yoichi have disappeared after having survived the effects of the tape. The only person left who knows anything about the original events is a teenage girl named Masami Kurahashi (Hitomi Sato) who now resides in a mental hospital and hasn't spoken since witnessing the death of her friend at the hands of the angry spirit Sadako.

When Takano pays Kurahashi a visit, she notices a strange occurrence where images from the legendary tape appear on a television whenever Kurahashi enters the room. The girl is examined by Dr. Kawajiri (Fumiyo Kohinata), who offers the explanation of an energy transference between Sadako and Kurahashi. The theory is proven correct when Takano finally locates Reiko and learns that young Yoichi is suffering from the same affliction as well as exhibiting telepathic abilities akin to the ones Sadako possessed in life. They must now find a way to expel the negative energy of the vengeful Sadako and break the curse once and for all.

At the same time, there are two subplots unfolding. The first involves Dr. Heihachiro Ikuma (Dr. Nagao in the books), played by Ban Daisuke), the man responsible for Sadako's death at the well years earlier. Ikuma must now make good by destroying Sadako's remains discovered by Reiko at the end of the first film.

The second involves a television reporter named Okazaki (Yurei Yanagi) who joins up with Takano to help solve the mystery of the video. He eventually receives a copy from a girl named Kannae (played by singer Kyoko Fukada) who begs him to watch it before her week is up. How she knows the secret to breaking the curse is anyone's guess.

It's a bit of confusing mess, albeit an interesting one that draws very little material from the second book in the series. The rules established in the first *Ringu* involving Sadako and the videotape are mutated and never fully explained. We are given lots of possibilities but no solid conclusions as to how exactly Sadako's curse works. It's clear that her influence is no longer confined to the videotape but exactly how she transfers her energy to people is left a mystery.

Sometimes it's the tape that kills, just like in the first film. Sometimes people don't die at all, but instead go crazy because there is a little bit of Sadako left inside their psyche. In a post-pandemic world, we might see the Sadako in *Ringu 2* as Long Covid. Ultimately, even Sadako doesn't understand why she can't be freed from the curse.

Logic aside, the film successfully manages to recreate the creepy atmosphere of its predecessor, though it lacks the overall tension and effective climax. It's sort of like a Rubik's Cube. You think you're close to figuring it out and then one little piece of the puzzle reveals itself as out of place, thwarting the solution. At this point you can either walk away from the puzzle or become obsessed with figuring it out. Judging from the number of web sites dedicated to the *Ringu* series it seems that a lot of people took the latter road. It's a credit to the manipulative genius of the filmmakers. *Ringu 2* is frustratingly ambiguous, but still engaging enough that you'll probably want to spend your hard-earned cash on the third installment of the series. The curse continues…

AUDITION (1999)

Good horror/suspense films are often like car wrecks. You don't like what you're seeing, but you just can't look away. Taking in the carnage may get you just a little closer to that dark part of the human psyche that - for most of us - lies out of reach. Takashi Miike excels at movies that fall into this category. He fully embraces the Jungian shadow of his characters and himself as an artist.

Some say he's a "David." Half David Cronenberg and half David Lynch. But I say he's all Takashi Miike. Quite possibly insane in the best possible way. *Audition* is not even the grossest of Miike's output. For that, seek *Visitor Q* (2001), a film that deals with incest.

The story in *Audition* concerns a middle-aged widower named Shigeharu (Ryo Ishibashi), who has spent the years following his wife's death raising his son Shigehiko (Tetsu Sawaki) alone. He is a hard worker who likes to spend quiet evenings at home with Gangu the family beagle.

He eventually succumbs to the pressure put on him by his son and friends to start dating again and agrees to take part in a phony audition set up by a friend who works in the film industry.

The female actresses all believe they are trying out for a movie when they're really being screened as a potential mate for Shigeharu.

Over a few days, Shigeharu sees many women, all of whom seem to suffer from some form of personality disorder, sometimes with comical results. It seems that Shigeharu will never find a "normal" girl. No mention is ever made of how dishonest the whole thing is. This is where the movie starts to drag. Viewers may find themselves wondering where exactly it's going. Trust me. When it gets to its final destination, it's worth your patience.

Finally, Shigeharu meets Asami (Eihi Shiina.) Asami is a shy slightly depressed woman who appears to be old-fashioned. She'd make a wonderful wife for Shigeharu. Or would she? Asami "gets the part" and the two begin dating under false pretenses. Asami eventually falls for Shigeharu. That's when the trouble begins.

Around the time Shigeharu proposes marriage, director Takashi Miike begins intercutting flashbacks showing that Asami is anything but normal. She was horrifically abused as a child by her wheelchair-bound dance instructor and she keeps her last boyfriend in a burlap sack in her apartment. He is, putting it delicately, no longer physically intact. She keeps him alive by feeding him her own vomit.

Asami insists on Shigeharu following a specific rule within their relationship. He must love her and *only* her without exception, including family. When Asami suspects that Shigeharu has broken the rule, she dons a butcher's apron and rubber gloves and punishes him.

Everything that happens in the apartment at the end of the film eradicates the slow pacing of what came before it. Essentially it's all been a slow ascent to the tallest, scariest roller coaster on earth. Without the long set up, the rest of the film wouldn't pack the punch during the insane descent that it does.

The final act contains images so disturbing that they may permanently etch themselves into the viewer's brain. There are long needles and piano wire. If you love beagles, this film is probably not for you. *Audition* has the ability to not only make the viewer feel uncomfortable, but filthy. You might feel like you need a shower after watching this excellent thriller. You have been warned. If you're like me (and I know I am) watch it anyway. It's an amazing exercise in WTF, which is what Miike does best.

ANOTHER HEAVEN (2000)

Directed by Jôji Ida, the man responsible for writing the TV version of *Ringu*, *Another Heaven* (2000) is a movie love child infused with the DNA of Kiyoshi Kurosawa's *Cure* (1997), Jack Sholder's underrated gem *The Hidden* (1987) and the masterpiece that is *John Carpenter's The Thing* (1982.)

The film begins as a typical murder mystery. Police officer Manabu Hayase (Yosuke Eguchi) and his superior, Inspector Tobitaka (Yoshio Harada) are called to the scene of a bizarre murder.

The victim has had his brains removed from his skull and cooked in a stew that's still boiling on the stove when the officers arrive. Initially, there are no leads, but eventually their investigation points to a college student named Kimura (Takashi Kashiwabara) who turns out to be a single piece of much larger puzzle.

An unknown creature is entering the brains of the Tokyo's citizens and forcing them to commit grizzly acts of murder. Kimura is only the latest host for the "something" that is moving from person to person, killing along its travels.

Sometimes the invader is an alien similar to the one in *The Hidden* and at other times it is a time-traveling pure evil organic element that reflects humanity's negative qualities. The being, whose nature and origin remain vague, endows its hosts with superhuman strength and athleticism. It also brings with it a headache so powerful, the hosts require nothing less than morphine to dull the pain. The entity must jump from body to body quickly before the host brain develops ulcers and disintegrates.

It is an intelligent and curious creature that soon sets its sights on Manabu, who shares its fascination with the dark side of humanity. While it's not clear exactly what the alien stands to learn from Manabu that it can't from anyone else, Manabu's redemption through the sweet but clingy Asako (Miwako Ichikawa) is an emotionally satisfying beat.

The tone is lighter than expected for a film in this genre with quite a few humorous moments throughout. The best dramatic moments occur when Manabu and Tobitaka are trying to identify the creature's current host. No one is to be trusted and their co-workers in the police department continually dismiss their wild claims. Tension and irony intertwine each time they discover the identity of the latest host. The films leaves audiences with many unanswered questions but overall, it's an enjoyable, well-directed piece of filmmaking largely overlooked from the second golden age.

VERSUS (2000)

Versus sucks you in immediately with simple but effective exposition. "There are 666 portals that connect this world to the other side. These are concealed from all human beings. Somewhere in Japan exists the 444th portal.... the forest of resurrection."

The action begins in the past. A samurai in feudal Japan fends off a group of zombies. After defeating them, he finds himself in the middle of something bigger. A battle between their powerful human leader and a mysterious stranger.

Flash forward to the same location, present day. We join two escaped prisoners on their way to liaise with five unknown Yakuza benefactors. At the meetup, prisoner KSC2-303, the only character given anything close to a name played by Tak Sakaguchi, is leery of the gangsters. Why would they help total strangers break out of jail? Even the gangsters don't know, yet. They're just following orders.

As tensions rise, we discover the Yakuza are holding a young lady (Chieko Misaka) hostage. There is an instant connection between the girl and Prisoner KSC2. A gun fight breaks out and several people end up dead (or in this case undead.) KSC2 and the woman flee together deep into the forest of resurrection where everyone who dies turns into a zombie.

The movie serves up a buffet of mayhem. We are treated to several wonderfully choreographed fight scenes, plenty of hilarious posing, outrageous gore and lots of zombie gun fights, one of which features the zombies themselves firing the weapons. If that doesn't sell you on this film, nothing will.

The various story lines come together when the gangsters' boss reveals himself to be the superhuman leader of the undead from the battle in the beginning of the film. Of course, he's bent on opening the 444th portal. KSC2 is his good-hearted brother, and the kidnapped woman is KSC2's reincarnated lover whose blood holds the power to open the portal.

Director Ryuhei Kitamura teases us not once, but three times with the possibility of a spectacular swordplay showdown between the two brothers. Each time, he diverts the action in another direction. When the battle does finally come to fruition, it's a corker filled with tightly composed hand-held shots and lightning fast cuts.

Upon its release, it was not only one of the best of the second golden age of Japanese cult cinema, but one of the best action-comedy gore films produced in a very long time in any nation. It stands proudly in the ring alongside heavyweights *Evil Dead 2*, and *Dead Alive* in the bloody laughs department.

The kinetic energy of the opening duel provided by the constant swirling camera sets the tone for the entire film. *Versus* looks like a John Woo film on speed with attractive actors and actresses being treated to more glamour shots than you can point two pistols at.

This is the film that got Ryuhei Kitamura noticed. He went on to direct *Godzilla: Final Wars* for Toho in 2004 and transitioned to Hollywood starting with the 2008 horror film *The Midnight Meat Train*. The sequel to *Versus* has been in development limbo since 2013, no doubt caught between realms. Hopefully, it will rise soon.

THE HAPPINESS OF THE KATAKURIS (2001)

This film is a true genre-buster. A black comedy and a horror suspense musical all rolled into one heart-warming tale about a family's struggle to open a guesthouse in the countryside.

The Katakuris are an urban family trying to build a new life together by leaving the city and opening a mountain retreat. There are, however, more than a few problems. The main road scheduled for construction near the *White Lover's Inn* doesn't exist yet and so guests (and their money) are few and far between.

To make matters worse, the people who do patronize the establishment have a nasty habit of dying often in comedic ways including a Sumo wrestler who suffers cardiac arrest while having sex with a schoolgirl, suffocating her in the process.

Instead of telling the police, the family opts to protect their dream and together, they bury all of the deceased guests in the nearby woods in order to avoid scandal. Intermittently, the family breaks into song and dance. The '80s and '90s style pop, rock songs and sugary sweet ballads all serve to develop the characters and flesh out the family dynamics.

Father Masao (Kenji Sawada) and mother Terue (Keiko Matsuzaka) are devoted parents and very much in love. Their son Masayuki (Shinji Takeda) is troubled and has a bit of a shady past.

Their daughter Shizue (*Godzilla 2000's* Naomi Nishida) is a love-starved divorced single mother.

Shizue is so lovelorn she falls in love on sight with the film's best supporting character, con-artist Richard Sagawa, who claims to be an illegitimate member of the British Royal Family. In the role, raspy-voiced rock singer Kiyoshiro Iwamano is a joy to behold. Especially during screendom's single best interpretation of bowel distress ever filmed.

There's also the loveable Grandpa Katakuri (played by the legendary Tetsuro Tamba) and his beloved dog Pochi, as well as Shizue's young daughter who narrates the film from an off-screen adult perspective.

Thematically, *The Happiness of Katakuris* (a remake of a Korean film titled *Quiet Family)*, waxes philosophical on some very interesting ideas involving mankind's place in the universe and how we persevere through life's adversities as a species. We are born, we live, we die and then it starts all over again. Family is everything.

It's a multi-layered, cross-genre film that defies all categorization and seamlessly combines the hysterically funny with the scary while remaining dramatically heart-wrenching. The sudden transitions from clay-mation to live-action are, at times, a little jarring but it's so creatively inspired that it's an absolutely pleasure to watch.

The world that Takashi Miike has created here is a bizarre one, but it's not an uncomfortable place. Japan's green mountain countryside is beautiful and the family's love for each other shines through even in their darkest moments. The Katakuris are regular people trying to build their family dream. They are easy to identify with despite their frequent lack of good judgement. We want them to succeed.

Takashi Miike is a mad genius. Even if he never made another film after this one, *The Happiness of the Katakuris* would have gone down in the history books as being one of the most ambitious and enjoyable films to come out of the second golden age.

DARK WATER (2002)

Dark Water isn't one of my favorites from the second golden age but I'm including it in this book for two reasons. First, because it had a successful remake released in the U.S. starring Jennifer Connelly in 2005. Second, because it has regained relevancy in recent years due to its striking similarity to an actual missing persons case uncovered in the 2021 *Netflix* documentary *Crime Scene: The Vanishing at the Cecil Hotel*.

In *Dark Water*, a newly divorced mother and her daughter move into an old apartment building haunted by the spirit of a little girl who was abandoned and died there.

Yoshimi Matsubara (J-drama star Hitomi Kuroki) is involved in a bitter custody battle with her ex-husband over their six-year-old daughter Ikuko (Rio Kanno.) While a court deliberates on the matter, Yoshimi and Ikuko move into a run-down apartment building and attempt to build a new life.

At first, things seem fine save for the annoying leaky ceiling in the bedroom. As time passes, the leak gets worse. The sound of dripping water goes from bothersome to overwhelming, similar to the segment *A Drop of Water* in Mario Bava's anthology chiller *Black Sabbath* (1963.) Even weirder, Ikuko starts talking to an imaginary friend named Mitsuko.

It's soon revealed that Mitsuko (Mirei Oguchi) was a missing child who lived in the apartment upstairs. Her ghost has returned because of the terrible injustice that caused her death. She wants to take Ikuko away with her but Yoshimi will protect her daughter at all costs.

Yoshimi has some childhood abandonment issues of her own stemming from her own parents' split. Consequently, she wants nothing more than to be a good mother to Ikuko, and to keep them together.

When Yoshimi uncovers the story of ghost Mitsuko's maternal abandonment, Yoshimi realizes to her horror that it's not Ikuko's company Mitsuko desires but her own. Ikuko is actually in the way.

Now she must choose between being Ikuko's mother and Mitsuko's. Surprisingly, her decision fulfills the needs of both children.

Dark Water shares many characteristics of Nakata Hideo's other hit film *Ringu* but *Dark Water* has a much better screenplay. Here, he accomplishes in two hours a depth of character for the ghost Mitsuko what took two films to do with Sadako in the *Ringu* series.

Mitsuko is given plenty of backstory. She's a tragic and potentially dangerous spirit who serves as a metaphor for Yoshimi's own inner child.

Japanese ghost stories rarely have happy endings. There are rarely straight up good guys and bad guys. Only flawed humans and regretful actions. Where *Ringu* ended on an anticlimactic note with the curse continuing, *Dark Water* features a satisfying albeit melancholy conclusion where we visit Ikuko ten years after the events and receive vicarious closure through her eyes. The conclusion will likely have more of a cathartic impact on viewers who come from divorced families. Do any of us ever truly heal from the fracturing of family?

Nobody knows how to build quiet tension the way Nakata does. His skill as a director and the convincing performance of lead Hitomi Kuroki convincingly turns something innocuous as a child's book bag into an ominous and terrifying object. We are never shown Mitsuko's face but instead are allowed only glimpses and quick shots.

Sound effects and music play a big part in creating the chilling mood of this film. The scene where Mitsuko pounds on the inside of the water tank was one of the most effective uses of sound I've ever witnessed.

If you're curious about the Cecil Hotel case, it doesn't involve a divorced mother or her abandoned child but the similarities are otherwise striking. Canadian tourist Elisa Lam went missing mysteriously only to be found inside the water tank on the roof of the building. How did she get there? We might never know. Some employees and guests believe her mysterious death explains all the reported supernatural goings on at that hotel since then. While not as creepy, the documentary makes a wonderful companion piece for *Dark Water*.

THREE EXTREMES (2004)
TAKASHI MIIKE'S BOX

A horror anthology in the tradition of Mario Bava's *Black Sabbath* (1963) and *Kwaidan* (1964), *Three Extremes* (2004) features three short stories directed by a trio of top directors working in Asian cinema at the turn of the 21st century.

The American Lions Gate release changed the order of the shorts from *Box* (directed by Takashi Miike)/*Dumplings* (directed by Hong Kong's Fruit Chan), and *Cut* (directed by South Korea's Park Chan-wook) to *Dumplings*/*Cut*/*Box*. Given that Miike's short is the strongest and weirdest of the three stories, the latter version is, in my assessment, superior.

Box revisits several themes Miike previously explored in *Audition* five years earlier, including isolation and child abuse. Both Asami from *Audition* and sisters Shoko and Kyoko in *Box* were childhood ballerinas who experienced sexual abuse at the hands of their benefactors.

Miike also incorporates elements familiar to fans of David Lynch involving twins, and their use in exploration of identity. Also like Lynch, Miike blurs the lines between dreams and reality expertly. The visual and auditory remain front and center while its story keeps the audience guessing from the first to the last shot.

The film opens with a series of disjointed images. A 25-year-old unnamed author dreams someone has wrapped her in a plastic bag and placed her inside a box. Above ground, we see a man burying the box in a rural winter setting.

During the day, she meets with her publisher Yoshii (Atsuro Watabe) in an abandoned building where the ghost of her sister Kyoko dwells. Yoshii, who looks suspiciously like a man from the author's traumatic past, tries to get the woman to open up to him without luck.

The narrative unfolds through the opening dream sequence repeated several times. Each time the protagonist dreams, Miike reveals a bit more of the sisters' history in reverse.

In childhood, 10-year-old Shoko and her twin sister Kyoko performed as circus ballerinas/assistants for an illusionist named Higata (Atsuro Watabe.) Higata's big finale is a trick where he places the girls' tiny bodies into boxes on either side of the stage.

It's clear the illusionist is a pedophile from the way he gazes at the nape of Shoko's neck as she contorts into position. He closes both lids and throws darts at the boxes. Upon impact, they each burst open, revealing white roses in one and red roses in the other.

Both girls performed identically (and perfectly), but Shoko is Higata's favorite. After the show, he gives her a necklace and praises her while Kyoko is left alone feeling jealous.

The favoritism bestowed upon Shoko by Higata becomes truly extreme when Kyoko finds them sleeping together in a loving embrace. In a dark twist, she is not upset because it's horrifying. She is heartbroken that it isn't her.

Kyoko accidentally kills Shoko in a fire when she locks the favorite twin inside one of the stage boxes, intending to take her place in Higata's bed for a single night.

The final reveal elicited loud gasps from the crowded theatre where I saw this film. In reality - at least I *think* it's reality - Shoko and Kyoko are conjoined twins and the entire film has been a series of dreams in the minds of the two characters. Kyoko grew into an adult. She serves as the main body while Shoko remains a

10-year-old girl attached to her sister's side. It is never explained how two conjoined twins could age at different rates.

Publisher Yoshii is real, but each twin dreams of him as Higata, the desirable tormentor. Of course, it's entirely possible the final reveal of the conjoined twins is also a dream. In that case, one could interpret the entire piece as a representation of what happens to sibling girls where one is sexually abused and the other is not. It deals with the feelings of resentment and a child's misinterpretation of predatory favoritism and the conflicting emotions involved.

In theory, such abuse would have halted the victim's emotional growth from the age at which the abuse occurred. Meanwhile, the physical body continues to maturity. It's disturbing as hell as far as last images go.

I'll never forget the looks on the faces of the people in the audience when the lights came up at the end of *Three Extremes*. As a conclusion to the trilogy of stories, *Box* leaves viewers in a state of wonder and wondering. The film is beautiful to look at it but, like so many of Miike's films, is also disconcerting.

The best horror films are the ones that make audiences feel something. I drove home that night haunted by what I'd seen, trying to sort out the various pieces of his cinematic puzzle and reassemble them in logical way. Miike knows the rules of the medium well enough to break them evocatively. It's what makes him one of the greatest, most consistently weird filmmakers of the second golden age.

SOLVING FOR X IN KIYOSHI KUROSAWA'S CURE

A SEMIOTIC ANALYSIS AND REVIEW

As a director of over 40 titles in his home country of Japan, Kurosawa Kiyoshi (no relation to Kurosawa Akira), is largely known in the west for his horror films. Born in Kobe in 1955, a generation after the great Japanese post-war filmmakers such as Suzuki Seijun and Fukasaku Kinji, he was educated at Rikkyo University where he studied Sociology. An apt subject for a man so interested in exploring the nature of humanity in his art.

He began making films in the early 1980s for the straight-to-video market but did not come to the attention of the international film circuit until his 15th feature, *Cure* (1997) screened at the Toronto Film Festival in 1998.

His success and reputation abroad continued to build from there with Kurosawa enjoying screenings of subsequent films at the Berlin, Cannes and Venice film festivals.

Critics and film scholars haven taken joy in analysing his films (Stephens, 2001), describing them as "existentialist" (O'Rourke, 2005), and "ambiguous" (DesJardins 2005, 214.) The use of these terms is fitting. Visually, his films are often filled with bleak urban landscapes devoid of human populations despite being shot in the crowded city of Tokyo.

On his soundtracks, he regularly employs a mixture of silence and ambient sound, evoking a sense of uneasiness, even in his non-horror genre fare.

Even more enigmatic are the plots, which often pose dilemmas for the protagonists and offer commentary on the problems of modern Japan. Nevertheless, his conclusions frequently offer no clear solutions for either, leaving audiences with more questions than answers.

Thematically, the films in his oeuvre invite many different interpretations. Critical analysis often focuses on the issues of "communication breakdown and isolation followed by the search for a new identity" (Rosenbaum 2010, 121.)

The fact that his films frequently explore these themes using the symbolism of earth, air, fire and water within the mise-en-scene has largely been overlooked.

I surmise a notion suggested by his mentor Shigehiko Hasumi (White 2007, 32) that, as a cinephile himself, Kurosawa, in exploring notions of identity on film via the elements of nature, is also exploring the very nature of the medium itself.

This analysis of *Cure* will be conducted using the semiotic approach known as the "third" or "obtuse" meaning pioneered by French philosopher Roland Barthes. Barthes's semiotic approaches, as well as cine-psychoanalysis, are considered canons in film theory.

Branded "perhaps the greatest critic of our epoch because of his responsiveness to texts, to culture" (Andrew 1984, 183), the Barthes brand of interpretation, is perhaps the most apt for the study of a filmmaker whose works so often feel obtuse.

The "third or obtuse meaning" constitutes the totality of the mise-en-scene (everything within the frame) as well as what an individual spectator brings to the proceedings. It is a concept as multifarious and difficult to disseminate as Kurosawa's films themselves.

In his 1970 essay titled *The Third Meaning*, Roland Barthes, when analyzing frames excised from Sergei Eisenstein's *Ivan the*

Terrible (1944, 1958), contended that films could be analyzed on three different levels.

The first level communicates information and messages to the audience through "the obvious," "…setting, costumes, the characters, their relations, their insertion in an anecdote…" (Barthes 1977, 52.)

The second level is that of symbolism, both referential and diegetic. He cites the use of gold in *Ivan The Terrible* (1944, 1958) as having two meanings (52.) One is the theme of wealth present within the film and the other is a reference to the "imperial ritual of baptism by gold" (52), which a spectator would have to bring into the viewing on their own as a reference, as Barthes does here. At this level, he also mentions symbolism specific to the filmmaker, in which a specific set of symbols can be interpreted throughout a filmmaker's body of work as having similar meaning (Barthes 1977, 52.) A modern example of this would include the reading of Quentin Tarantino's generous use of close-ups of feet as proof the director has a foot fetish.

The third level is "the obtuse" meaning. A meaning that cannot be described verbally. It encompasses the entirety of the mise-en-scene, the relation between the elements present within the frame as well as what an individual audience member brings to the interpretation because of their lived experience, culture, history and education. It therefore informs interpretation and at the same time "disturbs criticism" (61) in its fluidity.

"The obtuse" is not to be found in the structure of a film, but rather is movable within the narrative, and is an active process that occurs between a viewer and a film. It is "discontinuous, indifferent to the story and to the obvious meaning (as signification of the story)" (61.)

Barthes struggles to define it in his reading of Eisenstein and searches for ways to describe it which are inevitably peppered with the words "me", "my" and "I" while questioning the concept's very existence on a structural level (60-61.) Succinctly, it cannot exist without the active engagement of the spectator.

This "obtuse" meaning is the feeling I felt when first watching *Cure*. It's something I couldn't put into words, but I was transfixed by it.

The plot of *Cure* (1997) concerns Detective Takabe (Koji Yakusho) who spends his off-hours caring for his amnestic wife Fumie (Anna Nakagawa.) At his job, he becomes obsessed with solving an outbreak of random murders committed by seemingly upstanding citizens.

Although none of the perpetrators deny responsibility for their actions, in every case, their motive is vague and not a single one of them remembers what triggered their violence.

It turns out that a trigger is exactly what caused them to kill. During the investigation, Takabe uncovers that a young psychology student named Mamiya (Masato Hagiwara) has been employing hypnotic suggestion (invented by a man named Mesmer) onto random citizens, causing them to kill.[1]

It is soon revealed that Mamiya, like Takabe's wife, has amnesia. The first time we see him, he collapses on a beach. A passerby helps him and brings him back to his home. After regaining consciousness, Mamiya asks the man, "Who are you," while lighting a cigarette. For Mamiya, it's not a simple question.

In the next shot, Kurosawa uses the entire frame, as well as depth of field to convey the connection between fire and identity.

Now falling under Mamiya's spell, the helpful man remains in focus in the background on the left side of the frame. The lighter's out-of-focus flame, wielded by Mamiya fills up the right side. Mamiya is using fire as a hypnotic trigger to elicit the man's true nature.

The man answers Mamiya's question as any normal person would. He states his occupation and marital status. But, these are only aspects of his external identity. The man is incapable of digging deeper.

The day after encountering Mamiya, the man murders his wife and describes the act to Takabe as "the natural thing to do." Later, in a hospital, where Mamiya is forbidden from using his lighter, he adeptly switches to another natural element, that of water, in order to hypnotize a female doctor who also goes on to commit murder.

When Takabe is finally allowed to be alone with Mamiya, the two bond in a strange way. It's clear that Mamiya has used his hypnotic abilities on Takabe (again using water) but instead of making him kill right away, Mamiya chooses for him a special purpose to be revealed in the film's conclusion.

Why does he choose Takabe? Is it because Takabe's wife suffers from an ailment similar to Mamiya's? Maybe. It's more likely because Takabe is different. He doesn't answer Mamiya's questions by giving simple, surface-level responses. When Mamiya asks "Who are you?" Takabe opens up to Mayima and admits that his wife is a burden to him and that his life is full of frustration. Mamiya is fascinated by this.

Mesmer lives on through Mamiya either symbolically or literally depending on how the viewer perceives Mamiya's amnesia. He can't remember his own identity so he lives vicariously through exploring the identities of others. Most people answer his questions superficially, burying their true selves deep inside but Takabe possesses a self-awareness that captivates Mamiya. Takabe serves as the ultimate therapy patient to Mamiya's bored therapist. The paths of the two men inevitably become parallel.

In the meantime, a Dr. Sakuma (Tsuyoshi Ujiki) has discovered a videotape which contains very old footage of a woman being hypnotized by an unidentified man who gestures an "X" with his fingers. Is it Mesmer or one of his disciples? Yet another question to ponder long after the credits roll. There are a lot of those in *Cure*.

The fates of Dr. Sakuma, Detective Takabe and the mysterious Mr. Mamiya are best left revealed by the film, suffice it to say that they all discover their "true" selves and are "cured."

Author Jerry White finds implicit meaning in Kurosawa's use of water when he observes that the first time we see Mamiya on the beach, "it is as though he has just walked out of the ocean" (126.)

He does not see it as signifier to shifting identities, rather, as a birth metaphor (126), clearly forging the relation between spectator and film by bringing meaning to the shot, through his own extratextual cultural and educational knowledge of the symbolism of water.

White overlooks the additional elements of earth and air in this scene. For instance, Mamiya is wearing an earth-toned coat and is positioned to appear small in the center of the frame, completely surrounded by the sand of Shirasato Beach. The muted color palette of the shot gives the effect that Mamiya is a part of the landscape like a tree or a rock.

The blowing wind mixes with the rhythmic ebb and flow of the winter waves as an ever-present ambient hum of moving air on the soundtrack. It is a sound that Kurosawa repeats in subsequent scenes involving Mamiya, regardless of whether or not he is outdoors.

Since Mamiya can't remember his past, the viewer is left with nothing but the visual and auditory associations with which to interpret the identity of Mamiya as a personification of nature, capable of causing destruction in modern day Tokyo just as a hurricane might.

In his essay titled *Concepts of Nature: East and West*, Stephen R. Kellert posits, "Traditional Eastern attitudes toward nature often encourage passivity, even fatalism, toward a natural world depicted as all-powerful and beyond human capacity to control or grasp" (Kellert 1995, 117.)

The people who cross the path of Mamiya are in a sense, swept away by his mesmerism. Before they meet him, each person's true nature is repressed by their culture, which forces them to conform to society's rules. Once they fall under Mamiya's influence, their true identities emerge in an uncontrollable fashion, causing them to behave in a way they feel is "natural" in contrast to their daily lives.

Kurosawa articulates this duality between nature and Japanese society visually in the opening scene of the film, which I will interpret based on Barthes's three levels.

First, we see an average man walking to his destination accompanied by simple, upbeat music. The obvious meaning here is that the man is a normal, law-abiding citizen engaging in a normal day's activities.[2]

The second symbolic meaning begins when the man enters a traffic tunnel. The environment goes from light to dark, reflecting the man's internal nature. We see a close-up of the man's hand in a very quick cut-away, ripping a water pipe from its mount, disabling its normal function of carrying life-giving, cleansing water to people's homes. The breaking of the pipe allows the water to spill out from the broken conduit, metaphorically breaking the social infrastructure, allowing the natural element, representative of the true identity of the "typical" everyman to spill out.

In this sequence, the third meaning lies somewhere within the editing that begins to change pace in the tunnel. The sudden introduction of quick cuts feel like the equivalent of cinematic punches when compared to the longer preceding shots.

Particularly jarring is the cut to the close-up of the hand with the water spilling out. It feels important yet distracting due to its abrupt and short appearance. The insertion of this shot, with its precise length, taken in combination with the extra loud accompanying sound effect and implicit eroticism present in the liquid pouring forth from the phallic pipe, leaves the viewer with a feeling of uneasiness. There is nothing explicitly disturbing or sexual about the images. The notion comes out of the way the shots are combined.

This feeling disappears immediately with the next cut, rendering the viewing experience of the scene congruent with the theory postulated by Barthes, who argues that the third meaning is "…theoretically locatable but not describable" (64.)

Kurosawa Kiyoshi's mentor Shigehiko Hasmui exposed him to

many different kinds of films. [3] The quick insert of the breaking pipe could be Kurosawa creating his own cinephiliac moment as a filmmaker, harkening back to the jarring eyeball slashing in Luis Buñuel's *Un Chien Andalou* (1929.) An unforgettable moment for any first-time viewer.

Once again, it parallels Barthes who contends that, the indescribable fluid characteristic of the obtuse meaning is inherently "filmic" (Barthes 1977, 64) and can be "seen as the *passage* from language to *significance*... the founding act of film itself (65.)

If the obtuse meaning is inherently part of film language, then it can be concluded that Kurosawa, in his use of water throughout *Cure*, with its changeable characteristics, is not only exploring the identity of his characters onscreen, but is exploring the nature of film itself by creating moments that possess these characteristics.

White agrees when he states, "In Kurosawa's movies, film language and history are an intrinsic part of his thematic intentions, giving his work a complex, organic feel" (White 2007, 20.)

When questioned about his use of water as a hypnotic trigger leading to the revelation of a person's true identity by an audience member at a screening for the American Cinematheque in Hollywood,[4] Kurosawa ambiguously replied "I was mostly just interested in showing it as tasteless and transparent" (Desjardins 2005, 214.)

It is noteworthy that water shares many of the same changeable characteristics as the language of film as described by Barthes. In one state, water is fluid and transparent. It can take on the properties of a solid or a nearly invisible mist when subjected to different temperatures. It is mutable, just like the meaning of film. We could think of the varying temperatures that cause changes in water to be synonymous to the role of the spectator.

We can look at fire similarly. It can warm us, cook our food and power industry, or it can burn, maim and destroy.

Kurosawa's interest in mutability also reflects his concept of identity, which he expressed when he said:

> My sense of human life and human experience is that who I am today is not identical to who I am going to be tomorrow, and that we are slowly and subtly changing every day by the experiences we have. I think it's more natural to think of each of our human identities as quite fragile. Instead of finding it tragic that our sense of self and our identities might be changed profoundly by events that happen to us, I find in it hope and a different sense of self (DesJardins 219-220.)

Within the broader context of Japanese culture, changeability is a part of the general attitude towards nature. When questioned about his personal attitude towards nature at the same screening, Kurosawa confirmed:

> I think of nature as an alarming, terrifying, vast force that, at times, can beautiful and peaceful, but can just as readily come after you and devour you. So, far from human beings being above it, we're actually below it. I think the thing to do is leave well enough alone and not provoke nature. In that sense, I may be traditionally Japanese (DesJardins 219-220.)

The oppositional relationship of social constructs versus the true nature of mankind in *Cure* is evident in the decay present in its locations, which includes many dreary, abandoned buildings. These bleak landscapes, devoid of trees or any natural beauty, are representative of a greater crumbling of Japan's social infrastructure.

Author Chris DesJardins points out that Kurosawa shoots on "found locations rather than building artificial representations of the real world on sound stages (DesJardins 2005, 211.) He records the actors' dialogue on location and encourages his sound department to capture whatever sounds might be present on location such as "nearby rivers or construction sites" (213.)

Author Tim Palmer finds obtuse meaning in Kurosawa's use of abandoned locations as being what Barthes called "a signifier without a signified" (Barthes 1977, 61) when he says "The entropy aesthetic, then, emerges from a mise-en-scene of encroaching ruin, highlighted by Kurosawa's customary long shot/long takes of little tangible visual interest except for these memorably disused, crumbling backgrounds (Palmer 2010, 221.)

In *Cure*, this sense of emptiness within the frame, an "entropy aesthetic" is most obviously present in the abandoned warehouse hideaway of Mamiya. The dilapidated building, which is surrounded by the ever-encroaching woods, lies somewhere on the outskirts of Tokyo, although it is never specifically identified as to where. Significantly, it is in this rural location that Takabe comes to terms with his true self and is "cured" from the repression of social rigidity. He finds himself in a place where nature is growing over past human constructs and the same thing happens to him on a psychological level.

There is something surreal in this moment of the film, which remains fascinating no matter how times I watch it. It is intangible in Takabe's stride. His arms dangle limply at his sides. His slow gate embodies the obvious meaning of a detective suffering from exhaustion who has just concluded a difficult case. But there is something more in actor Yakusho's walk away from the camera.

Outwardly, the setting reflects ugliness and decay, but Yakusho's body language is so natural and peaceful that it evokes a feeling of calm, as though he is not acting at all, but simply walking through the frame while the camera happened to be rolling. It's the first time we see Takabe in stress-free state.

In this one shot, Kurosawa has captured the entire third meaning of the film when he explains:

> Urban dwellers in Japan are always shifting and waffling between their real selves and their social selves that they've created in order to survive in society. So, in that sense, when I capture the actor in the process of trying to become

the fictional character, I have, in fact, created the reflection of the typical Japanese urban dweller straddling the two" (DesJardins 2005, 213.)

I am fascinated with the moment when Takabe steps into the puddle of water during his walk. It signifies his submersion into his new identity. Other natural elements present in the shot include a soft breeze blowing through the broken window. A broken frame from the past through which people gazed out from their work at the freedom of their natural surrounding. A structure created by society, only to be subsequently abandoned and overtaken by the nearby trees, grass and soil.

This shot, more than any other in the film, sums up perfectly all of the themes discussed in this essay and encapsulates all of Kurosawa's representations of identity through earth, air, fire and water.

When asked about the more ambiguous moments in his films, like this one, the enigmatic director answered, "I never intentionally make ambiguous that which should be clear" (DesJardins 2005, 214.)

Clear from whose point of view? Kurosawa Kiyoshi's films defy one interpretation but invite many. That's what makes him great. *Cure* is a modern masterpiece.

I am in agreement with Barthes, who contends that each audience member brings their own point of view to the viewing experience, regardless of whether they are a scholar, critic, a filmmaker, student, or just a regular fan seeking out the best of Japanese cult cinema. This symbiotic relationship is not only the reason why I will continue to be a fan of Kurosawa Kiyoshi. It is the reason I will always be a cinephile.

AFTERWORD & ACKNOWLEDGEMENTS

I completed this book with a look at Kioyshi Kurosawa's *Cure* applying the Roland Barthes theory of the "obtuse" to find meaning. It occurs to me that non-fiction literary works such as this one are also dependent on the reader's background, their level of interest and knowledge in the subject.

Whether you've been watching Japanese cult cinema your entire life or you're just dipping your toes into the (dark) waters, I hope you've enjoyed this short, at times in depth look at some of my favorites from Japanese cinema's second golden age. I've enjoyed revisiting not only the films included, but choosing and retooling past academic essays and film reviews.

Until now, most of the work in this book enjoyed a quiet life on my computer's hard drive, waiting for me to summon them to crawl out from the screen like Sadako in *Ringu*. I promise, you won't die seven days from now.

Thanks to Adrian, Mom, Aunt Patty, Dianne, Fred, Bill, Sam, Julie and Jesse. For believing in my abilities as a writer, for giving valuable feedback and for providing hours of entertaining film discourse. You rock!

BIBLIOGRAPHY

Abe, Casio. 1994. *Beat Takeshi vs. Takeshi Kitano*. Translated from Japanese by William O. Gardner & Takeo Hori. New York: Kaya Press, an imprint of Muse Publishing.

Abe, Casio. 1999. "Kikujiro" in *'Beat' Takeshi Kitano*, 37-39. Edgeware: Tadao Press.

A Fistful of Dollars. 1964. [DVD] UK:Warner Home Video.

Akira Kurosawa's Dreams. 1990. [DVD] UK:Warner Home Video.

Alien. 1979. [DVD] Los Angeles: 20th Century Fox.

Aliens Special Edition. 1999. [DVD] Los Angeles: 20th Century Fox.

Andrew, J.D. 1984. *Concepts in Film Theory*. London: Oxford University Press.

Another Heaven. 2000. [DVD] Japan: Universe Laser & DVD.

Asia Pacific Arts. 2009. Interview with Kiyoshi Kurosawa. Viewed 25 July, 2012, <http://www.youtube.com/watch?v=3oLjNYTG0Ik>

Audition. 1999. [DVD] UK: Tartan Video.

Austin, Bruce A. 2006. "Portrait of a Cult Film Audience." In *The Film Audience: An Interntional Bibliography of Research, with Annotations and an Essay*. Lanham: Scarecrow Press.

Barthes, Roland. 1977. "The Third Meaning" in *Image, Music, Text*. Translated from French by Stephen Heath. London: Fontana Press.

Battle Royale. 2000. [DVD] UK: Tartan.

Black Sabbath. 1963. [Blu-ray] UK: Arrow Video.

Beller, Jonathan L. 2009. "Kino-I, Kino-World: Notes on the Cinematic Mode of Production" in *The Visual Culture Reader 2nd Edition*. Edited by Nicholas Mirzoeff. New York: Routledge.

Blake, Linnie. 2007. "Everyone Will Suffer: National Identity and the Spirit of Subaltern Vengeance in Nakata Hideo's *Ringu* and Gore Verbinski's *The Ring* in *Monstrous Adaptations*, edited by Richard J. Hand and Jay McRoy, 209-228. Manchester: Manchester University Press.

Bordwell, David. 1989. *Making Meaning: Inference and Rhetoric in the Interpretation of Cinema*. Cambridge: Harvard University Press.

Branded To Kill. 1967. [DVD] NewYork: The Criterion Collection.

Clover, Carol J. 1992. *Men, Women and Chainsaws: Gender in the Modern Horror Film*. Princeton: Princeton University Press.

Corrigan, Timothy. 2009. *A Short Guide to Writing About Film 7th Edition*. London: Longman Publishing.

Creed, Barbara. 1993. *The Monstrous Feminine: Film, Feminism, Psychoanalysis*. London & New York: Routledge.

Crime Scene: The Vanishing at the Cecil Hotel. 2021. [Streaming] USA: Netflix.

Cure. 1997. [DVD] Tokyo: Toshiba.

Daimajin. 1966. [DVD] UK: Arrow Video.

Dark Water. 2002. [DVD] Houston: ADV Films.
Dead Alive. 1992. [DVD] USA: Lions Gate.
DesJardins, Chris. 2005. *Outlaw Masters of Japanese Film*. London & New York: I.B.Tauris.
Doherty, Thomas. 1996. "Genre, Gender and the *Aliens* Trilogy" in *The Dread of Difference: Gender and the Horror Film*, edited by Barry Keith Grant, 181-199. Austin: University of Texas Press.
Evil Dead 2. 1987. [DVD] UK: Optimum Home Releasing.
Fiorini, Leticia Glocer. 2010. "The Analyst's Metatheories Concerning Sexual Difference and the Feminine" in *On Freud's Femininity*, edited by Leticia Glocer Fiorini and Graciela Abelin-Sas Rose, 79-96. London: Karnac Books.
Frankenstein. 1910. [DVD] USA: Ventures International.
Gamera: Guardian of The Universe. 1995. [DVD] UK: Arrow Video.
Gamera 2: The Advent of Legion. 1996. [DVD] UK: Arrow Video.
Gamera 3: Revenge of Iris. 1999. [DVD] UK: Arrow Video.
Gerow, Aaron. 2007. *Kitano Takeshi*. London: British Film Institute.
GMK: Godzilla, Mothra, King Ghidorah: Giant Monsters All-Out Out Monsters Attack. 2001. [DVD] USA: Columbia TriStar Home Entertainment.
Godzilla. 2014. [DVD] USA: Sony.
Godzilla: Final Wars. 2004. [Blu-ray] Germany: Splendid Film/WVG.
Godzilla 2000. 2ooo. [DVD] USA: Sony Pictures Home Entertainment.
Godzilla vs. Megaguirus. 2000. [DVD] USA: Columbia TriStar Home Entertainment.
Gojira. 1954. [DVD] Tokyo: Toho.
Gojira vs. Destroyah. 1995. [DVD] Germany: Laser Paradise.
The Grudge (Ju-On). 2002. [DVD] Tokyo: Cine-Asia Presents.
Hana-Bi. 1997. [DVD] UK: Momentum Pictures.
The Happiness of the Katakuris. 2003. [DVD] UK: Tartan.
The Hidden. 1987. [DVD] UK: Eiv.
Hills, Matt. 2005. "Ringing Changes: Cult Distinctions and Cultural Differences in US Fans' Reading of Japanese Horror Cinema" in *Japanese Horror Cinema* edited by Jay McRoy, 161-173. Honolulu: University of Hawai'i Press.
The Hunger Games. 2012. [DVD] USA: Lions Gate Home Entertainment.
Iles, Timothy. 2008. "Traveling Toward the Self in Japanese Film" in *The Crisis of Identity in Contemporary Japanese Film: Personal, Cultural, National*, 135-157. Leiden: Koninklijke Brill NV.
I Spit On Your Grave. 1978. [DVD) Los Angeles: Anchor Bay.
Ivan the Terrible. 1944. [Blu-ray) Russia. Bach Films.
John Carpenter's The Thing. 1982. [DVD] UK: Arrow Video.
Keathley, Christian. 2006. *Cinephilia and History, or The Wind in the Trees*. Bloomington & Indianapolis: Indiana University Press.
Kellert, Stephen. 1995. "Concepts of Nature East and West" in *Reinventing Nature? Responses to Postmodern Destruction*. San Francisco: Island Press.
Kikujiro. 1999. [DVD] Los Angeles: Sony Pictures Entertainment.
Kwaidan. 1964. [Blu-ray] UK: Eureka Entertainment.
The Magnificent Seven. 1960. [DVD] UK: MGM Home Entertainment.

Mes, Tom and Jasper Sharp. 2005. *The Midnight Eye Guide to New Japanese Film*. Berkeley: Stone Bridge Press.

McRoy, Jay. 2008. *Nightmare Japan: Contemporary Japanese Horror Cinema*. Amsterdam: Rodopi.

The Midnight Meat Train. 2008. [DVD] UK: Lions Gate.

Mulvey, Laura. 2006. "The Death Drive: Narrative Movement Stilled" in *Death 24 x a Second: Stillness and the Moving Image*, 67-84. London: Reacktion Books, Ltd.

Night of the Living Dead. 1968. [DVD] Los Angeles: Elite Entertainment, Inc.

"The 100 Greatest foreign-language films," in *BBC Culture* 2018. Viewed on 27 March, 2023, < https://www.bbc.com/culture/article/20181029-the-100-greatest-foreign-language-films>

O'Rourke, Jim. 2005. "Kiyoshi Kurosawa," *Bomb* Issue 91, Spring 2005. Viewed 14 May, 2012, <http://bombsite.com/issues/91/articles/2717>

Palmer, Tim. 2010. "The Rules of the World: Japanese Ecocinema and Kiyoshi Kurosawa" in *Framing the World: Explorations in Ecocriticism and Film*, 209-224. Virginia: University of Virginia Press.

Planes, Trains and Automobiles. 1987. [DVD] Los Angeles: Paramount Home Entertainment.

Princess Mononoke. 1997. [DVD] UK: Studio Canal.

Rebirth of Mothra. 1996. [Blu-ray] Los Angeles: Sony Pictures.

The Return of Godzilla. 1984. [DVD] Hong Kong: Universe.

"Revealed: the results of the 2022 Sight and Sound Greatest Films of All Time Poll," in *Sight and Sound Magazine* 1 December 2022. Viewed 23 March, 2023, <https://www.bfi.org.uk/news/revealed-results-2022-sight-sound-greatest-films-all-time-poll>

Richie, Donald. 2001. *A Hundred Years of Japanese Film*. Tokyo: Kodansha.

The Ring Box Office, 2012. Box Office Mojo. (online) Available at: <http://boxofficemojo.com/movies/?id=ring.htm> [Accessed 4 January 2012].

Ringu. 1998. [DVD] Los Angeles: Dreamworks.

Ringu 2. 1999. [DVD] Los Angeles: Dreamworks.

Rosenbaum, Jonathan. 2004. "Weird and Wonderful: Takeshi Kitano's Kikujiro" in *Essential Cinema: On the Necessity of Film Canons*, 313-315. Baltimore: The Johns Hopkins University Press.

Seven Samurai. 1954. [Blu-ray] New York: The Criterion Collection

Sonatine. 1993. [DVD] Los Angeles: Sony Pictures Entertainment.

Sontag, Susan. 1961. "Against Interpretation" in *Against Interpretation and Other Essays*. London: Penguin Classics.

Standish, Isolde. 2005. A New History of Japanese Cinema: A Century of Narrative Film. New York: The Continuum International Publishing Group Ltd.

Stephens, Chuck. 2001. "Kiyoshi Kurosawa Begins at the End: Out of the Woods," *The Village Voice* 24 July 2001. Viewed 26 July, 2012, <http://www.villagevoice.com/2001-07-24/film/kiyoshi-kurosawa-begins-at-the-end/ >

Stringer, Julian. 2007. "The Original and the Copy: Nakata Hideo's *Ring* (1998)" In *Japanese Cinema: Texts and Contexts*, edited by Alastair Phillips and Julian Stringer, 296-307. London & New York: Routledge.

Suzuki, Koji. 2007 [2004] [1991]. *Ringu*. Translated from Japanese by Robert B. Rohmer & Glynne Walley. New York: Vertical, Inc.

Takako, Imai. 1999. "Born to Be Wild" in *'Beat' Takeshi Kitano*, 5-15. Edgeware: Tadao Press Publication.

Takako, Imai. 1999. "All About Takeshi's Mother and His Misdemeanors" in *'Beat' Takeshi Kitano*, 5-15. Edgeware: Tadao Press Publication.

The Tale of Zatoichi. 1962. [DVD] London: Artificial Eye

Tetsuo. 1989. [Blu-ray] UK: Third Window Films.

Thomas-Mason, Lee 2021. "From Stanley Kubrick to Martin Scorsese: Akira Kurosawa once named his top 100 favorite films of all time" in *Far Out Magazine*. Viewed 4 April 2023.

Three Extremes. 2004. [FILM] USA: Lions Gate.

Tokyo Story. 1953. [DVD] NewYork: The Criterion Collection

Twin Peaks. 1990. [DVD] UK: Paramount Home Entertainment.

Udo, Tommy. 1999. "Sonatine" in *'Beat' Takeshi Kitano*, 27-28. Edgeware: Tadao Press Publication.

Un Chien Andalou. 1929. [FILM] USA: Public Domain.

Versus. 2000. [DVD] UK: Palisades Tartan.

Violent Cop. 1989. [DVD] UK: Second Sight.

Visitor Q. 2001. [DVD] UK: Palisades Tartan.

White, Eric. 2005. "Case Study: Nakata Hideo's *Ringu* and *Ringu 2*" in *Japanese Horror Cinema*, edited by Jay McRoy, 38-47. Honolulu: University of Hawai'i Press.

White, Jerry. 2007. *The Films of Kiyoshi Kurosawa: Master of Fear*. Berkeley: Stone Bridge Press.

Williams, Linda. 1996. "When the Woman Looks" In *The Dread of Difference: Gender and the Horror Film*, edited by Barry Keith Grant, 15-34. Austin: University of Texas Press.

Williams, Tony. 2003. *The Cinema of George A. Romero: Knight of the Living Dead*. London: Wallflower Press.

Yojimbo. 1961. [Blu-ray] NewYork: The Criterion Collection.

Zatoichi. 2003. [DVD] UK: Arrow Drome.

NOTES

HANA-BI (1997)

1. Kurosawa named Hana-bi as one of his top 100 films of all time in Far Out Magazine.

ZATOICHI (2003)

1. In 1899, the newly formed Association of Japanese Motion Pictures, founded by Komada Koyo, sponsored an entire series of films of geisha dances, all filmed at the Tokyo Kabuki-za (Richie 2001, 18.)

TRAVEL AS AN EXPRESSION OF PERSONAL GROWTH AND IDENTITY IN SONATINE AND KIKUJIRO

1. The auteur theory, as spearheaded by Village Voice Critic Andrew Sarris contends that a director's vision is the key component to making a film, which is a work of art (Corrigan 2009, 77.)
2. On 22 August, 1999 Saki died peacefully. She was 95 years old. When Takeshi went to see her two weeks before her death, he called out, "Ma, Ma, Ma!" She didn't reply but Takeshi knew, "I'm sure she recognized me because she was staring at me. I know she was very old but she was my mother. I felt that I've lost something" (Takao, 1999, 71.)

LOST IN ADAPTATION

1. Clover cites Bruce A. Austin, *The Film Audience* and "Portrait of a Cult Film Audience." When she asserts "the constituencies typically break down, in order of size, as follows; young men, frequently in groups but also solo; male-female couples of various ages (though mostly young); solo 'rogue males' (older men of ominous appearance and/or reactions); and adolescent girls in groups" (Clover 1992, 5.)
2. Creed argues that in the horror film "identificatory processes are extremely fluid and allow the spectator to switch identification between victim and monster depending on the degree to which the spectator wishes to be terrified and/or to terrify and depending on the power of the various filmic (subjective

camera, close-up images, music) designed to encourage certain modes of identification above others (Creed 1993, 155.)
3. As the novel progresses, Ryuji's amoral view of the world helps Asakawa to uncover the truth about Dr. Nagao (Suzuki 2007, 220) as well as doing the majority of the physical labor when the two men begin hauling heavy buckets of mud out of the well in order to retrieve Sadako's bones (Suzuki 2007, 243-244.)

SOLVING FOR X IN KIYOSHI KUROSAWA'S CURE

1. This plot summary of *Cure* (1997) is a variation on an original article I wrote for Lovehkfilm.com in 2002.
2. Barthes defines the obvious meaning being the one that "presents itself quite naturally to the mind" (Barthes 1977, 54).
3. When describing Kurosawa's relationship with his mentor, critic Shigehiko Hasumi, Mes and Sharp state that "Hasumi not only inspired his filmmaking, it also shaped the way he looked at films, as way as his personal cinematic tastes. He adopted Hasumi's predilection for American genre cinema, with a preference for such action-men directors as Robert Aldrich, Don Siegel, Sam Peckinpah, and Richard Fleischer, as well as a liking for horror specialists like Tobe Hooper and John Carpenter. At the same time, European art film-makers like Jean-Luc Godard, Wim Wenders, and Eric Rohmer, who had themselves been weaned on American cinema, as well as U.S. mavericks like John Cassavettes, formed another considerable strand of influence on Kurosawa" (Mes and Sharp 2005, 93).
4. I was a member of the Cinematheque for over ten years. The audiences present at these screenings were comprised of film students and scholars as well as industry professionals and critics.

ABOUT THE AUTHOR

J.M. Upton is an emerging author, genre film critic and an experienced ghost writer. This is her first book.

An American (non-werewolf) in London with a background in broadcasting and film, she wrote her dissertation for the Centre for Film & Media Studies at the University of London School of Oriental & African Studies and received her M.A. in Japanese Studies.

As a ghostwriter, she works with people from all walks of life including charity workers, the disabled, film directors, business people, actresses, immigrants, house wives and former members of the military.

A member of The Society of Authors, and The Alliance of Independent Authors, she also works as an editor, proofreader and book coach.

To find out more please visit www.jennuptonwriter.com

www.ingramcontent.com/pod-product-compliance
Lightning Source LLC
Chambersburg PA
CBHW050438010526
44118CB00013B/1586